A "Dress Rehearsal" for Revolution

John Trenchard and Thomas Gordon's Works in Eighteenth-Century British America

Heather E. Barry

UNIVERSITY PRESS OF AMERICA,® INC.
Lanham • Boulder • New York • Toronto • Plymouth, UK

Copyright © 2007 by
University Press of America,® Inc.
4501 Forbes Boulevard
Suite 200
Lanham, Maryland 20706
UPA Acquisitions Department (301) 459-3366

Estover Road
Plymouth PL6 7PY
United Kingdom

All rights reserved
Printed in the United States of America
British Library Cataloging in Publication Information Available

Library of Congress Control Number: 2007927903
ISBN-13: 978-0-7618-3814-2 (paperback : alk. paper)
ISBN-10: 0-7618-3814-7 (paperback : alk. paper)

∞™ The paper used in this publication meets the minimum
requirements of American National Standard for Information
Sciences—Permanence of Paper for Printed Library Materials,
ANSI Z39.48—1984

For My Parents and Jeb

Contents

Acknowledgments vii

Introduction 1

Part I

1 Trenchard and Gordon: Two London Political Writers 13

2 Trenchard and Gordon's Works in the British North
    American Colonies 27
    Trenchard and Gordon's Works in Libraries 27
    Trenchard and Gordon's Works For Sale 30
    Reprinting of Essays from the *Cato's Letters* Collection in
      Eighteenth-century Colonial Newspapers 30
    Reprinting of Essays from the *Independent Whig* Series
      in Eighteenth-century Colonial Newspapers 39
    Reprinting of Sections from Gordon's *Discourses
      Upon Tacitus* 40
    Possible Readership of Trenchard and Gordon's Works 40

Part II

3 Trenchard and Gordon's Works in Massachusetts Newspapers
    Before 1760 51

4 Trenchard and Gordon's Works in New York Newspapers
    Before 1760 62

5 Trenchard and Gordon's Works in Pennsylvania Newspapers
    Before 1760 85

6	Trenchard and Gordon's Works in British North American Colonial Newspapers After 1760	103
Conclusion		113
Appendix 1	Trenchard and Gordon's Works For Sale in Colonial Newspapers	117
Appendix 2	*Cato's Letters* When and Where Reprinted in the North American British Colonies during the Eighteenth Century	121
Appendix 3	Newspapers where essays from *Cato's Letters* appeared From 1721–1776	127
Bibliography		133
Index		141

Acknowledgments

I owe many thanks to David Baird, John McClung, Stephen Sale, and Roger D. McGrath for helping me during the early stages of my education. I had a lot to learn and they all contributed greatly to my intellectual development.

Karl Bottigheimer, Donna Rilling, and Susan Scheckel deserve a special thank you for guiding me through my early work on this manuscript. Their comments were most helpful and greatly appreciated.

I thank my advisor, Ned C. Landsman, for his thoughtful comments. He has been instrumental in the creation of this work. I owe him a great deal.

I thank Elena JP Marts and Genevieve E. Miller for their valued comments during the editing process.

The community at St. Joseph's College has been a remarkably supportive group. I appreciate the Faculty Development Small Grants Program who awarded funds to enable me to complete this work. I owe a special thank you to Sister Margaret Buckley, Sister Mary Florence Burns, Sister Elizabeth Hill, and Sister Loretta McGrann and Linda Ryan for being such strong, successful, and supportive women.

I am grateful to the entire history department at St. Joseph's College for creating a stimulating and supportive environment. Seth Armus for being a model scholar, Marie Fitzgerald for carrying much of the service burden for our department, Steven Fuchs for his excellent sense of humor, Mark Hessler for his articulate comments on my work, and Monica Brennan for urging me to pursue scholarship. This department is the best I could ever want. I thank them all for being so good to me.

I thank Roy R. Pellicano for teaching me how to be both a teacher and a scholar and the importance of research based teaching.

I also must thank Fritz, Therese, Beatrice, and Christian Lauener for providing me with a beautiful place in Wengen to work and recuperate and taking such excellent care of Jeb, which allowed me to pursue my academic goals.

I am indebted most of all to my parents and my son for supporting me in my endeavors. My parents have stood by me through thick and thin and I can never repay them for what they have done for me. They are the hardest working people I know and they passed this way of life on to me. My son, Jeb, is an amazing boy who has put up with my endless hours of work. Thanks Jeb for being so good to me!

Introduction

John Trenchard and Thomas Gordon were both political writers who published in London during the early eighteenth century. Together they authored two serial sets of essays titled the *Independent Whig* and *Cato's Letters*. The *Independent Whig* attacked the high Church of England and Catholicism. The essays signed "Cato" attacked "unjust" governments on a wide range of issues and dealt with various aspects of political theory. Their essays emphasized the need for liberty, virtue, and the ability to defend oneself.

Trenchard, in addition, wrote several essays about standing armies. Gordon translated the works of *Tacitus* and *Sallust*, which included several hundred pages of political discourse. Trenchard and Gordon's works were well known in London and became popular in the British North American colonies. This study examines the use and influences of Trenchard and Gordon's works in eighteenth-century British America. The way the various colonies used Trenchard and Gordon's works provides insight into the political culture and its development in British America.

The study begins in British society where Trenchard and Gordon's writings first gained popularity. This section explores who these men were and how their works related to eighteenth-century British political culture. The second section focuses on specific ideas of Trenchard and Gordon that were prominent in the colonies. Since colonists only read selections from Trenchard and Gordon's works, their understanding of these treatises developed in a distinctly colonial context. This concept of what Trenchard and Gordon represented was different than in London. To track this development the availability of their works in the colonies and the reception they experienced in British America. Finally, this project concludes with an evaluation of precisely when Trenchard and Gordon's works appeared in particular colonies and the possible reasons why they were reprinted. Knowing how Trenchard and Gordon's essays were actually read, one will be able to understand what these works meant to colonists in British America.

As early as 1912, historians recognized the popularity of Trenchard and Gordon's works, *Cato's Letters*, in America. Elizabeth Cook was one of the first to call attention to their crossover success into the New World. Cook proclaimed that "*Cato's Letters* were popular enough in the colonies to be quoted in every colonial newspaper from Boston to Savannah...."[1] Bernard Bailyn considered *Cato's Letters* to be a significant contributor to the American philosophy of government. According to Bailyn, "*Cato's Letters* were printed again and again, referred to and quoted in every possible context, in every colony in America."[2] Likewise, Forrest McDonald has argued, "*Cato's Letters* [was] the most quoted book in all the American's pre-Revolutionary [literature]."[3] And Lance Banning declared that the *Cato's Letters* "collection became the most popular political work in colonial America."[4] Gary Nash, in his work *The Urban Crucible,* went so far as to argue that "John Trenchard and Thomas Gordon were the most important disseminators of ideas to Americans in the prerevolutionary generations."[5] Nash further announced that "their *Cato's Letters* were widely read and reprinted in the American press."[6] Edmund Morgan, in his work *Inventing the People*, claimed that the colonists in America were "avid readers of Trenchard and Gordon."[7] Pauline Maier in her book, *From Resistance to Revolution*, alleged that Trenchard and Gordon's Cato essays "were a classic for many Americans."[8]

In contrast to the very general statements of most scholars, at least one, Leonard Levy, has suggested what might lie behind Cato's reception. In his work, *Legacy of Suppression*, Levy was more specific about Trenchard and Gordon's influence in colonial America. Levy assured that the main contribution of the essays was the "daring and well-developed theory of free speech."[9] Quoting from one of the essays, Levy claimed that without the freedom of speech and press there could be "neither Liberty, Property, true Religion, Arts, Sciences, Learning, or Knowledge." Levy believed that the freedom of speech was the linchpin of Trenchard and Gordon's arguments found in *Cato's Letters*; but even Levy's evaluation of Trenchard and Gordon's works is limited to tracing the influence of a couple of their essays.[10] Levy did not comment on the other Trenchard and Gordon essays that influenced colonial America.

Throughout the twentieth century, the majority of early American historians considered the works of Trenchard and Gordon significant because of the content of their essays. Historians, therefore, tried and some attempt to put Trenchard and Gordon into categories by evaluating the philosophical foundation of their works. Some argued that Trenchard and Gordon turned to John Locke's works to write their essays. Others contended that Trenchard and

Gordon consulted James Harrington's works to write many of their essays, and, most recently, some scholars awarded the influence of Thomas Hobbes a prominent place in Trenchard and Gordon's works.[11]

The attempt by some historians to determine the philosophical foundation of Trenchard and Gordon's works has led them to entangle Trenchard and Gordon's works in the Lockean Liberalism versus Republicanism debate that has raged for decades. The debate began with the genesis of a different understanding of eighteenth-century politics than was previously believed. For the first part of the twentieth century, many historians agreed that John Locke's ideas were the underlying philosophical foundation of colonials living in the British North American colonies during the eighteenth century.[12] Scholars believed that Americans supported Locke's ideas of individual rights and rights deeply rooted in the protection of private property, and used Trenchard and Gordon's works to bolster their arguments.[13]

During the last forty years some historians questioned the validity of the immense influence of Locke's ideas during the eighteenth century. These historians found that people during the eighteenth century saw the world differently than these Lockean advocates. Some historians believed that colonists viewed the world through notions of "republicanism" or "civic humanism" rather than through Lockean constructs. This group de-emphasized Locke's influence and they asserted that eighteenth-century British people saw their duty as citizens to participate in public life and also to be virtuous. These new historians of republicanism de-emphasized the individual and held that a virtuous man was supposed to be concerned with the welfare of the public in total instead of being swayed by private and selfish ends.[14]

Both sides of the debate exploited Trenchard and Gordon's essays for evidence. Since Trenchard and Gordon quoted from John Locke and even mentioned his name, historians used the reprinting of their works as evidence supporting the claim that Americans were steeped in Lockean Liberalism or libertarianism. Supporters of the Lockean interpretation believed that American colonists received many of their lessons on Locke indirectly through Trenchard and Gordon rather than directly reading Locke's works.

The departure from the belief that Lockean Liberalism was the underlying philosophical foundation for colonists began with historian Caroline Robbins.[15] Robbins approached analyzing Trenchard and Gordon's philosophical foundation differently by treating their works as a whole, rather than by just taking ideas that had prevailed in America. She declared that Trenchard and Gordon's works were influenced not only by John Locke but also by Algernon Sidney and James Harrington. She argued that they were part of a group of "Real Whigs" or "Commonwealthmen" who were a small minority of dissenters among the many Whigs in England who opposed corruption.[16]

Robbins also affirmed that the "Real Whigs" rejected economic development that was occurring in Britain in the eighteenth century. Robbins contended that the "Real Whigs" never organized as a party because they rejected parties and factions, and believed they led to corruption. Robbins maintained that because the "Real Whigs" failed to organize as a party, they were ineffective in England. However, the ideas from these particular Whigs became very popular in America and found long-term efficacy there. Robbins, therefore, claimed that the Real Whigs were best known for transmitting their libertarian values to America. Robbins agreed that Trenchard and Gordon's essays that were based on the ideas from Locke were the most significant in the British North American colonies. In this sense Robbins did not depart from the idea that the liberal tradition was most significant in the colonies.[17]

A shift occurred by J. G. A. Pocock from a teleological approach to studying all political works even if they did not retain long-term significance. Pocock believed that earlier historians took Locke's ideas out of the context in which eighteenth-century people would have placed them. Pocock came to a different interpretation from Lockean liberals. He attempted to recreate the social and intellectual world in which eighteenth-century British people lived. Pocock created a phrase to facilitate the comprehension of the eighteenth-century mindset. "Civic humanism," Pocock argued, was how men viewed human nature and the role they should play in society. Pocock believed that citizens of a society viewed "human life in terms of participation in particular actions and decision, in particular political relationships."[18] Men who claimed to be virtuous, therefore, sought to suppress self-interest in favor of the commonweal. Civic humanism, Pocock advocated, was the world-view that colonists had, rather than a Lockean understanding of the world. A virtuous populace, Pocock confirmed, should be concerned with the public good, not with private and selfish ends.[19]

Pocock argued that one must assess Trenchard and Gordon's works through the lens of the eighteenth-century mindset. Pocock propounded, therefore, that Cato was "not primarily a constitutional theorist" because the authors believed that a "concept of virtue dictated a politics of personal morality."[20] Pocock's emphasis on understanding the language of eighteenth-century people is crucial to understanding why rhetoricians, such as Trenchard and Gordon, used particular terms and how they defined them. Pocock disagreed with Robbin's limited category of "Commonwealthmen" and avowed that there were two more inclusive groups that would serve historians. Pocock contended that the "Real Whigs" were not the only group protesting against the alleged corruption in society. Pocock suggested that Trenchard and Gordon were part of a group of "Country" theorists versus "Court" theorists.[21] Pocock claimed that both Country and Court theorists believed that the "constitution consisted in the balance maintained between its parts." The "Country" theorists, however, thought that balance needed to be "preserved by preserving the parts in independence of each other." The Court advocates, in contrast, "contended that the balance was between parts that were interdependent and must be preserved by keeping the interdependence properly adjusted."[22] Both positions defined "corruption" as the upset of the balance of the British government.

The two groups did not agree on when this balance was upset or how to remedy the unbalance. Pocock believed Trenchard and Gordon and many others had a common understanding of the world. They believed that Britons had liberty because the British government was mixed and therefore balanced. The balance was achieved by the sovereignty of the King, Lords, and Commons.[23]

Many historians find specific categories of liberalism and republicanism confining and realized that the eighteenth-century political world was too complex to be able to use one term to describe the worldview. Historian Isaac Kramnick attempted to rectify the debate when he explained how society changed through the eighteenth century. Kramnick said that most British citizens understood the world through the republicanism or civic humanist lens up until the 1760s. Lockean Liberalism prevailed in the colonies after the 1760s and into the next century. The majority of Trenchard and Gordon's essays were reprinted *before* the 1760s. Since their essays seem to be steeped in republicanism, the reprinting history suggests that the colonists had more of a republican worldview before the 1760s than after.[24] Joyce Appleby directly addressed the liberalism/republicanism debate in her book *Liberalism and Republicanism in the Historical Imagination*. Appleby asserted that in the eighteenth century some people did have a republican world-view. She argued, however, that not everyone saw the world through that lens. Appleby also stated that some people did not have "a language" to describe their understanding of the world.[25]

As one can see, there has been considerable debate about Trenchard and Gordon's main philosophical foundation. Trenchard and Gordon were strong advocates of public virtue in order to preserve the free government in England. If republicanism is defined as the belief that people must be virtuous for a government to be free, then colonists who reprinted Trenchard and Gordon advocated this from 1720 to the Revolution. If republicanism meant that colonists equated a necessary virtuous populace with a republic, then Trenchard and Gordon's work would not have been influential. Trenchard and Gordon were advocates of mixed government, but not republics.[26]

Evidence suggests that historians have been short sighted in their interpretations. Historians have either been teleological, assessing Trenchard and Gordon's works by recognizing only what had a lasting effect on American society, or they have looked only at the sum total of their works, evaluating their works as a whole. Only a select number of Trenchard and Gordon's works, however, were read by the literate public in the British colonies; those that the Americans reprinted did not convey a consistent philosophical theory on government or society.

Historians were correct in noting that Trenchard and Gordon's works were reprinted in the colonies and that their works were influential. This study, however, attempts to be very specific about how, when, and where their works were used in the colonies. The popularity of Trenchard and Gordon's works can be evaluated by looking at the availability of their works and how often their works appeared in libraries, schools, personal papers, and newspapers.

Historians have exaggerated the number of times Trenchard and Gordon's works as a whole were reprinted. For example, fewer than half of these authors' 144 essays signed "Cato" were reprinted in newspapers between 1720 and the outbreak of the American Revolution. Newspapers in urban areas such as New York City, Philadelphia, and Boston reprinted more of Trenchard and Gordon's works than those in the southern areas, which only reprinted a very select few or none at all before 1760. The use of Trenchard and Gordon's works was conditional and selective, depending on the political culture of the different colonies. New York City, Philadelphia, and Boston printers published Trenchard and Gordon's works where newspapers were prevalent and used by political factions to advocate particular positions. More specifically, Trenchard and Gordon's works appeared precisely where the bourgeois public sphere was beginning to develop. As historian Jurgen Habermas indicated, the public sphere was where critical public discussion of matters of general interest occurred. Through the development of newspapers, which were no longer just a "vehicle for the transformation of information," the public sphere existed to the greatest extent.[27]

Michael Warner, in his work *The Letters of the Republic*, applied Habermas's study to eighteenth-century America. Warner argued that print and republican political culture mutually transformed each other. The public sphere, created by the rise of printing, enabled citizens to participate in their duty to be citizens, as the theory of republicanism indicates. Since republicanism was based on civic participation, newspapers and other print gave citizens an opportunity to take part in discussions that involved government. In turn, republicanism encouraged further printing of newspapers, pamphlets, and broadsides. Warner demonstrated how political essays such as Trenchard and Gordon's, found in newspapers, encouraged citizens to take part in government by keeping rulers or people in power in check.[28]

The historiography of print culture warrants attention since it establishes the importance of newspapers, which printed most of Trenchard and Gordon's works in the British colonies. Charles Clark's work, *The Public Prints*, argues that the colonies were "remarkably well served by newspapers."²⁹ He calculated that overall in 1740 a newspaper copy existed for every 125 colonists. He compared that to Great Britain as a whole where there was a copy for every 67. He also briefly mentioned there were regional differences in readership among the British colonies in America.³⁰ Furthermore, Kathleen Wilson held that provincial newspapers bound "men and women in particular ways to the wider political processes of the state, nation, and empire."³¹ Wilson argued that through newspapers, provincial towns created an extraparliamentary nation in which people could participate and where people could have a voice. Wilson also charts the growing interest of the reading public in national politics, which was facilitated by the increase of printed material.

Another contributor to the belief that the press encouraged middling sorts of people to become citizens and take part in government came from T. H. Breen. Breen specifically discussed the rise of Country party ideas in New England and argued that the largest contribution the Country party made to political life in New England was how they used the printing press to educate the public. Breen found that the "new role of the press entailed the principle of supervision, which exerted the force of discipline on the legislature."³²

Many colonial historians acknowledge Cato's significance; however, not much consideration is given to what was actually read or *how* Trenchard and Gordon's works were read. Historians assume that Cato was seen as a clear and unitary voice to which colonists responded. Therefore, this study examines Trenchard and Gordon's role in the various colonies where their works were reprinted. We will see that their works were not used uniformly throughout the colonies. Colonists who read Trenchard and Gordon's works probably did not all formulate the same conclusions. In some colonies, where the public sphere was well developed, readers received a filtered version of Trenchard and Gordon's ideas due to the fact that they were reading select essays in newspapers. In contrast, someone who knew about Trenchard and Gordon in the colonies where the public sphere was not well developed probably read Trenchard and Gordon in book form; he or she read either the entire collection or made the choice to read particular essays.

A closer examination of exactly when and where their essays were reprinted also casts doubt on the argument that *Cato's Letters* served as an ideological foundation for the American Revolution. In the colonies where Cato's essays were reprinted the most in number, such as in New York and Pennsylvania, there was much opposition to the American Revolution. In contrast, in Virginia, where Cato's essays were not reprinted in newspapers until the 1760s, people were the most unified in their support for the American Revolution.³³

The colonists did not reprint Trenchard and Gordon's works because they saw themselves entering into London's political discussions; Trenchard and

Gordon's works were reprinted at specific times for particular reasons that often revolved around local politics before the 1760s. The colonists reprinted a select number of Trenchard and Gordon's essays, and they usually reprinted them word for word and attributed them to Trenchard and Gordon. Colonists reprinted Trenchard and Gordon's works during local controversies because these essays were passionate, simple, and addressed popular topics of eighteenth-century society. In addition, because English common law did not give people the liberty to publish against government officials, Trenchard and Gordon's writings were "safer" for printers to reprint. Since their works were first printed in England, colonists were less likely to be sued for seditious libel for just *re*printing someone else's works.[34]

During the 1760s, Trenchard and Gordon's essays were reprinted in a wider range of newspapers, not just in opposition newspapers. Well-established colonial newspapers took on the role of opposition to the metropolis rather than to each other. For the most part, colonists during the 1760s read some of Trenchard and Gordon's works but probably without realizing the author's identity. A few ideas from Trenchard and Gordon converged into the colonists' vocabulary through quotation and probably conversation. Evidence shows that by the immediate pre-Revolutionary period, a few popularized quotes from Trenchard and Gordon became a part of the colonists' vocabulary, which was very different from the use of their works earlier in the century.

This work attempts to be more specific about the role Trenchard and Gordon's works played in British America. This study sets out to uncover the nuances that are involved in determining the role Trenchard and Gordon's works had in the colonies. Part I evaluates the overall use of Trenchard and Gordon's works in England and then in British North America. Part I places Trenchard and Gordon's works into the context of English society. Then, the general popularity of their works in the American colonies and their possible readership is revealed. Part II presents specifically when, where, and more specifically why particular colonists chose to reprint certain essays written by Trenchard and Gordon. In Part II the reader will understand how selections from Trenchard and Gordon's works entered into the political arena on particular occasions. The reader will have a better understanding of how Trenchard and Gordon's works influenced politics in eighteenth-century British America. The reader will also have a better understanding of the political culture of the various colonies by looking through the lens of Trenchard and Gordon's works.

NOTES

1. Elizabeth Christine Cook, *Literary Influences in Colonial Newspapers 1704–1750* (New York: Columbia University Press, 1912), 81. Bernard Bailyn quoted this same statement in his book from Cook. Bernard Bailyn, *The Ideological Origins of the Amer-*

ican Revolution (Cambridge, MA: Belknap Press of Harvard University Press, 1992), 36. Leonard Levy quoted the same statement in *Legacy of Suppression*, 120.

2. Bernard Bailyn, *The Origins of American Politics* (New York: Vintage Books: A Division of Random House, 1967), 54.

3. Forrest McDonald "A Founding Father's Library," *Literature of Liberty,* Vol. 1, No. 1 (January/March 1978), 113.

4. Lance Banning, *The Jeffersonian Persuasion: Evolution of a Party Ideology* (Ithaca, NY: Cornell University Press, 1978), 72.

5. Gary Nash, *The Urban Crucible: Social Change, Political Consciousness, and the Origins of the American Revolution* (Cambridge, Massachusetts: Harvard University Press, 1979), 348.

6. Nash, *The Urban Crucible*, 348.

7. Edmund S. Morgan, *Inventing the People: The Rise of Popular Sovereignty in England and America* (New York: W. W. Norton and Company, 1988), 167.

8. Pauline Maier, *From Resistance to Revolution: Colonial Radicals and the Development of American Opposition to Britain, 1765–1776* (New York: W. W. Norton and Company, 1991), 27.

9. Leonard W. Levy, *Legacy of Suppression: Freedom of Speech and Press in Early American History* (Cambridge, MA: Belknap Press of Harvard University Press, 1960), 116.

10. Levy, *Legacy of Suppression,* 318, 121, 116. Levy argued that Trenchard and Gordon did not merely praise freedom of speech and press "but they considered its values, meaning, and problems." Levy, 118.

11. Gary L. McDowell, "The Language of Law and the Foundations of American Constitutionalism." *William and Mary Quarterly*, 3rd Series, (July 1998) Vol. LV, No. 3. McDowell argued that Trenchard and Gordon's *Cato's Letters* and *Independent Whig* series "constituted two of the most basic texts of the colonial period. . . ." McDowell then contextually analyzed Trenchard and Gordon's essays and found that their works were supposedly heavily based on Thomas Hobbes's works. McDowell then proceeded to argue that Trenchard and Gordon's works were influential in the development of American constitutionalism.

12. Works that propounded the ultimate importance to John Locke and his ideas included: George M. Dutcher, "The Rise of Republican Government in the United States," *Political Science Quarterly*, LV (1940). Zera S. Fink, *The Classical Republicans: An Essay in the Recovery of a Pattern of Thought in Seventeenth Century England* (Evanston, Ill., 1945); Andrew C. McLaughlin, *The Foundations of American Constitutionalism* (New York: 1932); Carl Becker, *The Declaration of Independence: A Study in the History of Political Ideas* (New York, 1922).

13. Bernard Bailyn, *The Origins of American Politics* (New York: Vintage Books, 1968), 40, 43–44. Clinton Rossiter, *Seedtime of the Republic* (New York: Harcourt, Brace & World, Inc., 1953). Leonard Levy, *Legacy of Suppression*.

14. Bernard Bailyn, *The Ideological Origins of the American Revolution* (Cambridge, MA., 1967), and *The Origins of American Politics* (New York, 1967), 41; Gordon Wood, *The Creation of the American Republic, 1776–1787* (Chapel Hill, N.C., 1969); Pocock, *The Machiavellian Moment: Florentine Political Thought and the Atlantic Republican Tradition* (Princeton, N.J., 1975), and Pocock's article "The Machiavellian Moment Revisited: A Study in History and Ideology," *Journal of World History*, LIII (1981), 49–72.

15. Caroline Robbins, *The Eighteenth-Century Commonwealthmen: Studies in the Transmission, Development and Circumstance of English Liberal Thought from the Restoration of Charles II until the War with the Thirteen Colonies* (Cambridge, MA: Harvard University Press, 1961), 115–121. Caroline Robbins, however, still placed the philosophical foundation of Trenchard and Gordon within a "liberal" tradition, which limits their philosophical foundation.

16. Robbins, *The Eighteenth-Century Commonwealthmen*, 115–125.

17. Robbins, *The Eighteenth-Century Commonwealthmen*, 115–125.

18. Pocock, *Machiavellian Moment*, 58–60.

19. Pocock, *Machiavellian Moment*, 58–60.

20. Pocock, *Machiavellian Moment*, 470.

21. The Country and Court categories helps rectify the similarities of works by Tory supporter Viscount Bolingbroke with some Whigs such as Trenchard and Gordon. In Bolingbroke's *Craftsman*, Trenchard and Gordon's *Cato's Letters* series was quoted several times even though they were of two opposing political groups. Caroline Robbins's category of "Real Whigs" limited the group to a select type of writers and eliminated people who had similar interests.

22. Pocock, "Machiavelli, Harrington and English Political Ideologies in the Eighteenth Century," *William and Mary Quarterly* 3rd Series, Vol. 22, No. 4 (Oct 1965), 571.

23. Pocock, "Machiavelli, Harrington and English Political Ideologies in the Eighteenth Century," 549–583 and *Machiavellian Moment*, 426–427.

24. Isaac Kramnick, *Republican and Bourgeois Radicalism: Political Ideology in Late Eighteenth-Century England and America* (Ithaca, NY: Cornell University Press, 1990), 165.

25. Joyce Appleby, *Liberalism and Republicanism in the Historical Imagination* (Cambridge, MA: Harvard University Press, 1992), 21–23.

26. Trenchard and Gordon made their position throughout their essays. See specifically *Cato's Letters* Numbers 14, 68, and 85.

27. Jurgen Habermas, *The Structural Transformation of the Public Sphere: An Inquiry into a Category of Bourgeois Society* (Cambridge: The MIT Press, 1991), xi–xiv and 183.

28. Michael Warner, *Letters of the Republic: Publication and the Public Sphere in Eighteenth-Century America* (Cambridge, MA: Harvard University Press, 1990), 64–65, 76.

29. Charles E. Clark, *The Public Prints: The Newspaper in Anglo-American Culture, 1665–1740* (New York: Oxford University Press, 1994), 259.

30. Clark, *The Public Prints*, 259.

31. Kathleen Wilson, *The Sense of the People: Politics, Culture, and Imperialism in England, 1715–1785* (Cambridge, UK: Cambridge University Press, 1995), 37.

32. T. H. Breen, *Character of a Good Ruler: A Study of Puritan Political Ideas in New England, 1630–1730* (New Haven, CT: Yale University Press, 1970), 247, 58.

33. Jack P. Greene, "Society, Ideology, and Politics: An Analysis of the Political Culture of mid-Eighteenth-Century Virginia," in Richard M. Jellison, ed., *Society, Freedom, and Conscience: The American Revolution in Virginia, Massachusetts, and New York* (New York, 1976), 14–76.

34. Ned C. Landsman, *From Colonials to Provincials: American Thought and Culture 1680–1760* (New York: Twayne Publishers, 1997), 37–39.

Part I

Chapter One

Trenchard and Gordon: Two London Political Writers

John Trenchard and Thomas Gordon began their writing careers separately and eventually met and formed a partnership. Trenchard was born in 1662 in Dublin into a locally respected family.[1] He studied law at Trinity College, Dublin. He worked as a barrister for a short time and in 1690 he served as commissioner for forfeited estates in Ireland. He soon became wealthy from inheritances from his uncle and father. Trenchard married a woman who had considerable property, which resulted in Trenchard's large estate. Trenchard then was able to devote himself to writing on contemporary politics.

Trenchard became well known in London as a result of the essays he published during a controversy over standing armies that occurred in London from 1697 to 1699. During this three-year period, debates took place in parliament and in the press regarding standing armies. One side argued in favor of a standing army in order to defend the nation if necessary. Another group favored a reduction of the army, and a third group argued for getting rid of the standing army entirely while the nation was not engaged in war. The latter two groups argued that standing armies were a threat to public liberty; therefore, the power of the army should be decreased or removed completely.

Historians regard John Trenchard as the leader of the pamphleteers who opposed a standing army during peacetime.[2] Trenchard's first pamphlet that initiated the controversy was titled: *An Argument, Shewing, That a Standing Army Is Inconsistent with a Free Government, and Absolutely Destructive to the Constitution of the English Monarchy*. Then in December of 1697 he published *A Letter from the Author of the Argument against a Standing Army*, to the *Author of the Ballancing Letter and The Second Part of an Argument . . . with Remarks on the Late Published List of King James's Irish Force in France*. In November of 1698, Trenchard wrote his most popular pamphlet titled *A Short History of*

Standing Armies in England. This tract went through three editions in 1698, and the preface was reprinted in whole or in part more than eight times during the eighteenth century.[3] This pamphlet supposedly agitated the administration more than any other work during the controversy.

Trenchard argued that standing armies were dangerous to a country in times of peace. Trenchard stated that a king could use a standing army to encroach upon the liberties of the people. Trenchard gave examples from history of how standing armies often led to arbitrary governments—governments dictated by the whim of an absolute power. Trenchard and his supporters were not able to persuade Parliament to rid the country of the standing army. The antimilitary tracts, however, did alert the public to the dangers of standing armies in peacetime and made it difficult for King William to increase his military.

Thomas Gordon's past is more ambiguous than Trenchard's. The date of his birth is unknown, but some think he was born in Kirikcudbright, Scotland near the end of the seventeenth century. We do not know whether he received a formal education. There was a Thomas Gordon who graduated from King's College in 1713. Historians have also found a Thomas Gordon who submitted a law thesis at Edinburgh in 1716. In addition, there is some evidence that suggests that Gordon lived in Wiltshire, England in 1718 and was there teaching languages.[4]

The first concrete information about Gordon was that he published a piece in 1718 titled: *A Dedication to a Great Man Concerning Dedications.* Then in 1720 he published a series of ironic essays titled: *The Humorist.* Gordon's next literary venture made him better known in London--his essays written during the "Bangorian controversy." Benjamin Hoadly, the Bishop of Bangor, initiated the controversy in 1717 by making statements that criticized church authority, contending that the church should not have power over an individual's conscience.[5] Some church officials responded to Hoadly in defense of the power of the church. Accordingly, others responded to the church's position and supported Hoadly's statements.[6] Since Gordon argued in favor of Hoadly, against the Church's authority, his works attracted the attention of John Trenchard. They then began their partnership as co-authors.

In 1719, Trenchard and Gordon met and produced *The Character of an Independent Whig,* which became the first section of the *Independent Whig* collection.[7] The essay revealed Trenchard and Gordon's anticlericalism, anti-Jacobitism, fear of standing armies, and their sympathy for persecuted Protestants.[8] This first part went through at least four editions in London. In the last section, the authors stated that they planned to continue to publish essays regularly from the "Independent Whig." The collection of essays signed the *Independent Whig* totaled fifty-three by the time it ended. The essays were printed individually from 20 January 1720 to 5 January 1721. Gordon authored twenty-two of the essays, Trenchard wrote eighteen; both jointly penned three of them, and an unidentified author wrote ten.[9]

Records indicate that the *Independent Whig* collection was reprinted at least fifteen times throughout the eighteenth century. London publishers reprinted the series more than ten times. The collection was also reprinted in the British North American colonies, Ireland, and Amsterdam.[10]

Trenchard and Gordon wrote the *Independent Whig* series to express their fear of standing armies, Jacobitism, anticlericalism, and to argue for the rights of Protestant dissenters. Jacobites were people who wanted to overthrow the Hanoverian reign and replace the British monarchy with the Stuart dynasty. The Jacobites had connections to Roman Catholicism because the last ousted Stuart monarch, James II, was Roman Catholic. The *Independent Whig* essays, therefore, attacked the Roman Catholic Church for encouraging conspiracies to overthrow the British monarchy. Trenchard and Gordon called the Roman Catholic Church tyrannical and dangerous to Britain as a sovereign nation.

Most of the essays that comprised the *Independent Whig* series discussed the dangers associated with the hierarchical nature of the Anglican and Roman Catholic churches along with the unjust actions of church officials who persecuted Protestant dissenters. In essays III, V, XIV, XVIII, and XIX Trenchard and Gordon argued that any religion that upheld an ordained clergy was corrupt and "wicked."[11] They believed that any group who preached that they were above another was dangerous to society because it denied people the truth. In essay XVIII, the *Independent Whig* asserted that: "priests of all religions have kept their craft and impostures from a discovery, and made the Truth, as far as they could inaccessible." More specific to the Anglican Church, the *Independent Whig* wrote: "Ecclesiastical authority, as claimed by the High clergy, [was] an enemy to religion."[12] They believed that the word of God, as revealed in the *Bible,* should be open to laymen and not kept as a secret message only for church officials to decipher.[13]

The *Independent Whig* series included essays that criticized the use of ceremonies in churches (especially in the Anglican Church) and the alleged hypocrisy of the Catholic traditions of celibacy and the power of the Pope.[14] Several essays, including numbers VIII and XXIV addressed the persecutions of Protestant dissenters. Essay XXIV stated: "To punish men for opinions that are even plainly false and absurd, is barbarous and unreasonable."[15] The author continued to claim that persecution was a "war of craft against conscience" and "we ought then constantly to oppose all claims of Dominion in the clergy; for they naturally end in Cruelty."[16]

Trenchard and Gordon also addressed the subject of reason. They averred that "reason [was] the only guide given to men in the state of nature, to find out the will of God, and the means of self-preservation."[17] Furthermore, they contended that "reason checks tumultuous passion, the greatest enemy to the peace of the mind, and to the peace of society." Trenchard and Gordon summed up their perspective when they encouraged Englishmen to support a freethinking Protestant religion where people were guided by reason and were free to judge for themselves.[18]

After the *Independent Whig* series ended in January of 1720, Trenchard and Gordon began a series of essays that addressed the alleged corruption of the British government. Trenchard and Gordon published their essays, at first, in the *London Journal,* and then published the remaining essays in the *British Journal*.[19] Trenchard and Gordon decided to sign their essays "Cato." The name was probably chosen for a couple of reasons. First, the name Cato was chosen in memory of the ancient Roman, Cato the Younger who lived from 95–46 B.C.E. Cato the Younger had opposed Julius Caesar and was famous for his commitment to republican principles. Cato had come to be seen as a martyr for republican ideas in the eighteenth century because he sacrificed his life in the name of liberty. Cato committed suicide rather than live in a place where liberty did not prevail. Second, the name Cato became popular after Joseph Addison published a play about the trials and victories of liberty and public virtue and named the play *Cato*. This play was well known in Britain and in the British North American colonies.[20]

Trenchard and Gordon were not the only authors who wrote polemic works to vent their political frustrations in eighteenth-century London. Some historians labeled writers such as Trenchard and Gordon as "Real Whigs." Real Whigs were a dissenting group of political writers who believed that British liberties were in danger and this group held a similar understanding of the government and how it should function in Britain. The Real Whigs formed partly in response to the rise of a different kind of politics that began to be openly practiced in the eighteenth century, which the whigs considered to be corrupt and incompatible with free governments. The Real Whigs eventually opposed some of the actions taken by the administration.

The issue of corruption joined some Real Whigs and anti-Jacobite Tories[21] together because both were opposed to corruption.[22] One of the most influential voices for the non-Jacobite Tories was St. John, Henry, Viscount Bolingbroke and his newspaper *The Craftsman*. *The Craftsman* "attacked Walpole's direction of all the offices of government: army, commerce, foreign alliances, and revenues."[23] Bolingbroke quoted from Trenchard and Gordon on several occasions because they all were opposing the administration. Bolingbroke, however, was not fond of Gordon's works as indicated by Bolingbroke's comment upon hearing of Gordon's death. Bolingbroke called him the "worst" writer in England.[24]

Some historians believe that Trenchard and Gordon did not continue to oppose the Walpole administration for very long. Due to the content of their essays it seems that they changed their position and became supporters of the administration and eventually Gordon worked for the Walpole administration.[25]

Trenchard and Gordon opened their Cato series with an attack on the administration for its involvement in the South-Sea Stock Company crisis. This crisis was a popular topic for discussion in London during the 1720s since the crash agitated England's economy. The South-Sea Company was created in 1711 by the Tory Earl of Oxford, Robert Harley.[26] He attempted to alleviate England's national debt amassed during the former wars with France and Spain. Harley hoped to tap into potential resources in South America by creating a British monopoly over the trade. He then wanted to pay off the national debt by making the company a financier. The South-Sea Company was not very successful because of unforeseen problems with trading with South American countries.[27] In 1719, the company forged a deal with Parliament to assume the national debt. For a little over a year the stock in the company steadily increased because it attracted many investors from the extremely wealthy to the very poor. Soon people began to realize that they overextended themselves and because many bought on margin, there was a rush to sell back the South-Sea stocks. This led the price of the stock into a precipitous decline, which ended in a panic. This panic was so great some government officials thought it was necessary for the government to help the company and its investors out of their financial problems.

Trenchard and Gordon began their series with several essays that addressed the South-Sea Bubble Crisis. They used this opportunity to attack people who were involved in buying and selling stocks. These "stock-jobbers," as Cato referred to them as, were a "dirty race of money-changers."[28] Cato believed that government officials should not participate in schemes that involved setting stocks, giving monopolies, or any other "deceitful" activity. Trenchard and Gordon referred to these actions as corrupt because these activities only benefited a few people in society at the expense of the general populace. To them, these types of activities threatened what they considered to be free government in England.[29]

This discussion led Trenchard and Gordon to explain their philosophy on how free governments could exist. They argued that free governments could exist only if there were virtuous people in power. A virtuous person, as defined by eighteenth-century Englishmen, was someone who suppressed self-interest in favor of the public good. The conflict that Trenchard and Gordon recognized was that people did not have a natural predilection to act virtuously. In deed, they believed that people in power positions had a propensity to be corrupt in order to gain as much power as possible. Trenchard and Gordon, therefore, preached that "the people," which to them were land-owning independent people,[30] had to force government officials to act virtuously. They argued that people must demand that leaders make decisions that were good for the commonweal. Cato explained that "the people" had a duty to support virtuous government officials and also to expose corrupt officials. Trenchard and Gordon attempted to persuade the people that their duty to expose corruption was necessary in order for liberty to prevail in England. Trenchard and Gordon explained the essential need for the freedom of speech in order for the people to have the proper mechanism to perform their duty of protecting liberty by exposing government corruption.[31]

After these essays on their philosophy on government, Trenchard and Gordon returned to their original subject, the government officials who participated in the South-Sea Bubble. Cato argued that because some members of Parliament were involved in the scheme, they threatened English liberty. Since they held positions of power and they abused their positions to benefit a portion of the public, the people involved in the scheme threatened the public good. The participants in the scheme, moreover, argued that they acted in the best interest of the public and explained that the scheme was an attempt to decrease the national debt. This justification disgusted Trenchard and Gordon and they stated that this excuse was typical because corrupt men deviously try to explain their actions in the name of virtue.[32]

Furthermore, Trenchard and Gordon argued that corrupt government officials were more dangerous to English liberty than Jacobites. They explained that Jacobites *openly* attacked the government and liberty.[33] Jacobites made their intentions clear; they wanted to restore the Stuart dynasty. Cato held that the Jacobites could not acquire enough support because most people in England enjoyed the liberty that English government protected, and therefore, the Jacobites were not nearly as threatening to English liberty as corrupt people who threatened free governments by wearing away slowly at the liberties of the people.

In several other essays, Trenchard and Gordon expressed their views of government monopolies and again they protested the government's plan to alleviate the South-Sea Company's financial crisis. Their objection to monopolies was situated within their philosophy on government. Monopolies, they asserted, benefited only a part of the commonweal, and since they believed that free governments must make policies only in favor of the whole people, monopolies threatened liberty. Trenchard and Gordon considered the South-Sea Company to be a monopoly and warned the public about the dangers to liberty that would result from the government helping the South-Sea Company with their financial situation.[34]

The South-Sea Company was not mentioned in the remainder of the collection. The subjects of the last forty-six essays reiterated Trenchard and Gordon's philosophy of government. The majority of the essays included further discussions of liberty, virtue, human nature, and gave instructions on how to preserve liberty. A virtuous populace must curb a man's insatiable desire for power, in order to preserve liberty.

The content of Cato's essays changed slightly after the Atterbury plot of 1720–1722 was exposed in 1723.[35] The plot, headed by Bishop of Rochester, Francis Atterbury, was an attempt to replace the Hanoverian monarchy with the Catholic Stuart heir to the throne, James Francis Edward, son of James II.

Atterbury and his conspirators planned an armed rebellion to overthrow the monarchy. This plot divided the Jacobite Tories in England. Some Tories participated in the plot, some stayed aloof from it, and others were unaware of the plan. For various reasons, the plot failed and the administration became aware of the people involved.[36]

The plot revived anti-Jacobite sentiments among some people in England including Trenchard and Gordon. Trenchard and Gordon expounded upon the alleged tyrannical power of the Church of Rome in twelve essays. They attacked the clergy and the practices of the Catholic Church in a manner similar to that in the *Independent Whig* series of essays. They explained how free government could never exist in Catholic nations because the religious doctrines of the Church of Rome were dictated to the people. Trenchard and Gordon further explained that their philosophy of free governments was incompatible with Catholicism.

The last Cato essay, titled "Cato's Farewell," reiterated Trenchard and Gordon's philosophy of government. They alleged that men instituted civil governments, and property-owning men had a duty to take part in the dealings of government in order to preserve liberty. This last essay was a plea for men to defend what Trenchard and Gordon considered the most liberty preserving empire on earth.

Cato's Letters had a wide distribution in England during its first appearance in the *London Journal,* since more than eight thousand copies of the newspaper were distributed per week while the collection appeared.[37] *Cato's Letters* was printed in London in 1721 and 1722 and titled: *A Collection of Cato's Letters* and *Political Letters in the London Journal.*[38] Then the series went through six editions of a complete four volume set under the title: *Cato's Letters: Or, Essays on Liberty, Civil and Religious, And other Important Subjects.*[39] The *Cato's Letters* series was also translated into Dutch and French and published in Amsterdam and Paris respectively in the eighteenth century.[40]

Trenchard and Gordon wrote their last essay together and published it on 27 July 1723. Soon after, Trenchard died from what Gordon called an "ulcer of the kidneys."[41] Gordon published six additional essays signed Criton, which became part of the *Cato's Letters* series in later editions.

After Trenchard's death, Gordon married Trenchard's widow and thereby acquired his substantial estate. Gordon then received a post as commissioner of wine licenses, which he kept until his death in 1750. Along with his post, Gordon continued to write. Some historians suggest that the Walpole administration bribed Gordon, causing Gordon to cease opposing the government.[42] Other historians argue that Gordon was already allied with Walpole before he received his position in the administration. After reading the entire collection of *Cato's Letters* one is led to believe that Trenchard and Gordon were not entirely against the Walpole administration. They opposed some of the ways the government was functioning under Walpole, mainly the relationship between government officials and stock companies. They did not advocate an overthrow of the government but a change in some of the policies that they believed were a threat to British liberty.

Once the South-Sea Company crisis was over, Trenchard and Gordon no longer addressed the issue and they discussed other topics that were popular at the time of publication. The essays indicate that they did not change their philosophy of government but they discussed different alleged threats to free governments.

While Gordon held his position as wine commissioner, he wrote an extensive introduction and then translation of the works of *Tacitus*, which was dedicated to Walpole. Gordon's *Tacitus*, as it became known, went through at least seven editions in Europe and included thirteen essays that discussed governments that were free and others that he considered arbitrary.[43] He dedicated seven essays to examples of what happened when unlimited power was given to someone or to some group. He then discussed, in seven more essays, freedom of speech and human nature.[44] The remaining six essays explained the dangers of standing armies to the liberties of people living in a free nation.

At first glance the essays that comprised Gordon's *Discourses upon Tacitus* seem similar to the essays included in Trenchard and Gordon *Cato's Letters* series. Gordon did not change his philosophy but the *Discourses* reads more like a history textbook than political argument. Gordon included essays that discussed the essential role laws contributed to free societies, problems with corruption in free governments, and the importance of limited monarchies. Gordon included only a few lines with a current political topic and then the remainder of the essay consisted of a history lesson.

For example, Gordon included an essay on the freedom of speech in his *Cato's Letters* series and in his *Discourses upon Tacitus*, but the two read very differently. The essay in the Cato series began with the following statement: "Without the freedom of thought, there can be no such thing as wisdom; and no such thing as public liberty, without freedom of speech. . . ."[45] The essay continued with similar fiery certainty. In contrast, the essay on the freedom of speech stated more indirectly: "During those Reigns which I have been describing, when power was established in terrors, and subjection converted into abasement, small was the wonder that restraint upon speech was no inconsiderable link in the public chain. . . ."[46] Gordon's later work lost some of the passion that was used in the *Cato's Letters* series. The essays that comprised Gordon's *Discourses Upon Tacitus* also lost some of the radical oppositional nature of his *Independent Whig* and *Cato's Letters* essays. This seems reasonable since Gordon's earlier works were written for occasional publication in newspapers—not in a timeless book.

Gordon worked also on a translation of the works of *Sallust*, which went through at least five editions.⁴⁷ He included two hundred pages of discourse in which he expounded upon politics and society. In three essays Gordon discussed the danger of factions in a free society. Eight essays addressed human nature, three essays described the dangers of corruption, and seven essays were devoted to the civil wars. In addition, Gordon wrote eight essays on the mutability of government.

Gordon discussed in great detail the dangers of participating in party politics in a free society. He warned that party politics led to people supporting others only because they were part of a party. He explained that men must support only people who acted in the best interest of the commonweal instead of for self-interest.

Gordon, in his essays on human nature, contended that it was natural for men to acquire as much power as they could. Anyone or any group given "boundless power" would soon possess absolute power. Gordon then gave examples of men who were in power who betrayed the public trust and continued to do so until the public forced them to stop. Gordon's last eight essays, in his *Discourse upon Sallust* section, advocated the need for government to be changeable so that as society changed, government could adapt and still function effectively. Governments, where liberty prevails, needed to have an element of mutability.⁴⁸

Historians have noted the popularity of Trenchard and Gordon's works on the European Continent during the eighteenth century.⁴⁹ Gordon's *Tacitus* and *Sallust* were more popular on the Continent, than their other works. Several philosophers, such as Voltaire, Grimm, Mirabeau, and Desmoulins, commented on how they admired Gordon's translations.⁵⁰ Gordon's *Tacitus* and *Sallust* were translated and published in Geneva, Amsterdam, and Madrid.⁵¹ His *Sallust* was translated into French and published in 1759. His *Tacitus* and *Sallust* were both reprinted during the French Revolution.

Trenchard and Gordon's *Independent Whig* series was also popular on the Continent, mainly due to the subject matter. The essays that comprised the *Independent Whig* attacked the Catholic Church and clericalism, which were controversial issues throughout Europe. Particularly in France, sections of the *Independent Whig* were translated and published under the title: *L'Esprit du clerge*. Baron D'Holbach, the French philosopher, was responsible for publishing some of Trenchard and Gordon's works in France. Historians have found that D'Holbach admired Trenchard enough to have borrowed his name and attached it to his own work, which was titled *La contagion sacree* in 1768.⁵²

Cato's Letters was not very popular on the continent. There were a few editions published in France and Holland, but the subject matter of *Cato's Letters* seemed unattractive to many publishers on the continent.⁵³ It is probable that the idea of balanced government led by virtuous leaders did not fit well into the French idea of government. Before the French Revolution, the government of France was a so-called absolute monarchy bolstered by Catholicism. Then during the French Revolution, the government of France was democratic in nature and violent, which was not what Trenchard and Gordon advocated in their essays either.

In contrast, *Cato's Letters* was the most popular Trenchard and Gordon work in the British North American colonies. Their various works were present in many private and public libraries; and some essays were reprinted in newspapers, magazines, and pamphlets. For the purpose of this study, it is important to estimate how popular Trenchard and Gordon's works were in eighteenth-century colonial America.

NOTES

1. Trenchard was born the son of Sir William Trenchard who was a distant relative of Sir John Trenchard, secretary of state under King William. Lois G. Schwoerer. "The Literature of the Standing Army Controversy, 1697–1699." *The Huntington Library Quarterly* (May 1965) vol. XXCIII, Number 3, 187–212.

2. Lois G. Schwoerer. "The Literature of the Standing Army Controversy, 1697–1699." *The Huntington Library Quarterly* (May 1964) vol. XXCIII, Number 3, 189.

3. Trenchard's *An Argument* was reprinted in 1698, 1706, 1727, 1751, 1817.

4. J. M. Bulloch, "Thomas Gordon, The 'Independent Whig': A Biographical Bibliography," *Aberdeen University Library Bulletin* (1918) 598–612, 733–749.

5. First Benjamin Hoadly made his views known in a piece he wrote titled: *Preservative against the Principles and Practices of the Nonjurors* (London: Knapton and Childe, 1716) and in a sermon he delivered to the royal family in 1717 which he titled: "Nature of the Kingdom of Christ" (London: Knapton, 1717).

6. Thomas Gordon's essays included: *A Modest Apology for Parson Alberoni* (London: J. Roberts, 1717) and *An Apology for the Danger of the Church* (London: J. Roberts, 1719).

7. *The Character of an Independent Whig* (London: J. Roberts, 1719–1720). The *Independent Whig* collection was started immediately after the Duke of Ormonde from Spain supported a Jacobite invasion of Scotland. Spain had supplied the Jacobites with ten ships of war and six thousand troops for the invasion. The fleet, however, ended up scattered and defeated. This uprising spurred concern from many non-Catholic Englishmen; this concern was explicit in the essays that comprised the *Independent Whig* collection. Ronald Hamowy ed., *Cato's Letters: Or, Essays on Liberty, Civil and Religious, And other Important Subjects* (Indianapolis, IN: Liberty Fund, 1995), 622.

8. David L. Jacobson, *The England Libertarian Heritage* (San Francisco, CA: Fox & Wilkes, 1965), xxii–xxiii.

9. Jacobson, *The England Libertarian Heritage*, xxiv. Some suspect that Anthony Collins (1676–1729) authored ten of the essays. Collins was a friend and disciple of

John Locke and a well-known deistic writer. He published several works and some included *Priestcraft in Perfection* (1709), *Discourse on Free Thinking* (1713), and *Discourse on Grounds and Reasons of the Christian Religion* (1724).

10. *The Independent Whig* (London: J. Peele, 1721); (London: J. Peele, 1722). Second edition. (Philadelphia: S. Keimer, 1724). A partial serialization. (London: J. Peele, 1726). Third edition. (London: J. Peele, 1728). Fourth edition. (2 vols., London: J. Osborn, 1732–1735). Fifth edition. The numbering for the various editions in the 1730's is highly erratic. (3 vol., London: J. Peele, 1732–1735). An "enlarged" edition. (London, 1736). Seventh edition. Philadelphia: Bradford, 1740). (3 vols., London: J. Peele, 1743). Also called seventh edition. (4 vols., London: J. Peele, 1747). Includes three volumes of 1743 plus a fourth and new volume. (Dublin, 1748). A reprint of the greater part of the fourth volume of 1747). (Manchester, 1750). Selections from Trenchard and Gordon and other writers. (London: R. Ware, 1752). *L'Esprit du Clerge, ou le Christianisme primitif venge des enterprises et des exces de nos pretres modernes* (2 vol., London [Amsterdam]: Weller, 1767). A translation of *The Independent Whig* done by Baron D'Holbach.

11. *Independent Whig*, Numbers X and XI.
12. *Independent Whig*, Number XVIII.
13. *Independent Whig*, Numbers XVIII and XIX.
14. *Independent Whig*, Numbers XXXI, XXXII, "Of Ceremonies," and Numbers XXII and XXXIX against "Popish Priests."
15. *Independent Whig*, Number XXIV.
16. *Independent Whig*, Number XXIV.
17. *Independent Whig*, Number XXIV.
18. *Independent Whig*, Number XXXV, 14 September 1720.
19. The first essay of the *Cato's Letters* series was printed in the *London Journal* on 5 November 1720. The last essay was printed in the *British Journal* on 7 December 1723. The legal calendar in England until 31 December 1751 was the Julian, or Old Style, calendar, which was then eleven days behind the Gregorian, or New Style, calendar in use throughout the rest of Europe, except Russia.
20. Joseph Addison's play, *Cato, A Tragedy* ran through six editions in England in 1713, and another fourteen by the end of the century, not counting four editions published in Boston and Worcester, Massachusetts between 1767 and 1787. From Colbourn, 29. The work was also translated into Italian, French, and German. From William-Alan Landes ed. Studio City, CA: Players Press, Inc., 1996.
21. Anti-Jacobite Tories were people belonging to the Tory group that did not participate in Jacobite activities to try to overthrow the Hanoverian reign with the Stuart dynasty.
22. Kathleen Wilson, *The Sense of the People: Politics, Culture and Imperialism in England, 1715–1785* (Cambridge, UK: Cambridge University Press, 1995), 121.
23. Isaac Kramnick, *Republican and Bourgeois Radicalism: Political Ideology in Late Eighteenth-Century England and America* (Ithaca, NY: Cornell University Press, 1990), 112.
24. Jacobson, *The England Libertarian Heritage*, xxx.
25. Van Mobley. *The Consolidation of the First British Empire*. Dissertation 1999 University of Wisconsin-Madison.

26. The information regarding the South-Sea Company is from Virginia Cowles's *The Great Swindle: The Story of the South Sea Bubble* (New York: Harper and Brothers publishers, 1960). See also John Carswell's *The South Sea Bubble* (Stanford, CA: Standford University Press, 1960).

27. Harley hoped to establish a monopoly on the trade to South America. He planned to import slaves from Africa on a large scale to South America. He had hoped that more gold would be discovered there so that the slaves would be bought with gold. This gold would be brought back to England and in the eighteenth-century mercantile economy would have added wealth to the nation. In addition, he thought that the more settlers would go to the land and therefore open up markets for English goods to be sold. This is not what happened. Spain did not give England a monopoly on the trade to South America. In addition, transporting slaves from Africa proved to be an expensive venture. Many of the slave ships were lost to buccaneers, many slaves died en route, and others were smuggling slaves to South America, which drove the price of slaves down. For more information on the problems with the South-Sea Company see Virginia Cowles, *The Great Swindle: The Story of the South Sea Bubble* (New York: Harper and Brothers Publishers, 1960).

28. *Cato's Letters*, Number 2.

29. The South-Sea Company could have been targeted also, because unlike the private Bank of England and the East India Company, the South-Sea Company was granted a charter from a Tory Parliament and was governed from the beginning by a Tory directorate. Also, the Tories in government were trying to undermine the Bank of England, which was controlled by Whigs.

30. *Cato's Letters*, Number 16 defined what Trenchard and Gordon meant by "the people." "There are reasons too at hand, why ambitious men should grasp at the possession of immense wealth, high honours, and exorbitant power: But that the gentry, the body of the people in a free nation, should become tools and instruments of knaves and pick-pockets; should list themselves in their quarrels, and fight their battles; and this too, often at the expense, and by the violation of good neighborhood, near relation, private friendships: That men of great estates and quality, for small and trifling considerations, and sometimes none at all, should promote wild, villainous projects, to the ruin of themselves and country, by making precarious their own titles to their lives, estates, and liberties, is something so stupendous, that it must be thought impossible, if daily experience did not convince us that it is more than possible." The gentry were land-owning individuals. Trenchard and Gordon, along with many Englishmen, believed that only land-owning individuals could vote independent of outside influences. They thought that in order for a person to have the privilege to vote he then must be independent of others. Therefore, if a person worked for someone, he could be forced to vote a particular way because his livelihood depended upon it.

31. *Cato's Letters*, Number 16.

32. *Cato's Letters*, Number 16.

33. After the discovery of a clandestine Jacobite Plot—the Atterbury Plot—Trenchard and Gordon realize that Jacobites did not openly attack the government and they assert their threat in more severe terms.

34. *Cato's Letters*, Numbers 87–92.

35. The account of the Atterbury Plot is based on G. V. Bennett's *The Tory Crisis in Church and State 1688–1730: The Career of Francis Atterbury Bishop of Rochester* (Oxford: Clarendon Press, 1975), 223–275.

36. For specific reasons why the plot failed see Bennett's *The Tory Crisis*.

37. Charles Bechdolt Realey, "The London Journal and Its Authors, 1720–1723," *Bulletin of the University of Kansas* Volume V (1936), 1–38. Realey argued that the *London Journal* was the most influential in England from 1720–1723. The essays that appeared in the *Journal* were "among the most troublesome thorns that pricked the vulnerable sides of the British ministry."

38. *A Collection of Cato's Letters* (London: J. Roberts, 1721). A partial collection of the letters to December 17, 1720. This appeared in at least two editions, the second with a "new Preface." *Political Letters in the London Journal* (London: J. Roberts, 1721). A third partial collection included the letters published before the end of March, 1721. At least four further collections were published in 1721 and 1722 by J. Roberts and J. Peele.

39. *Cato's Letters* (4 vols., London: Wilkins, Walthoe, Woodward, and Peele, 1724). The first full collection. (4 vols., London: W. Wilkins, 1731). (4 vols., London: W. Wilkins, 1733). Third edition. (4 vols., London: W. Wilkins, 1737). Fourth edition. (4 vols., London: Woodward and Walthoe, 1748). Fifth edition. (4 vols., London: Walthoe, 1754–1755). The final, "corrected" edition from which the selections in this volume are taken.

40. *Brieven over de Vryheid en het Geluk des Volks onder pen Goede Regeerung in't Englesch uitgegeeven op den Naam van Cato* (3 vols., Amsterdam: Tongerlo, Houttayn, 1754). One hundred and thirty-three of *Cato's Letters* translated into Dutch. *Dix-septieme lettre de Caton, traduite de l'Anglais de Thomas Gordon* (Paris: A. Baudoin, [1790]). Translated by J. L. Chalmel.

41. Trenchard was sick for quite some time before he died. Some implied Trenchard had committed suicide, however, Gordon denied that in the Preface a *Cato's Letters* edition printed in London by Walthoe in 1755.

42. It was a common practice for government officials to bribe writers who published against the administration. It was less trouble to pay off the printers and writers than to sue them. Note that it was illegal to print against the government in England during the eighteenth century if the printed material could be proven to have undermined the authority of the government. Kramnick, *Bolingbroke and His Circle: The Politics of Nostalgia in the Age of Walpole*. Cambridge: Harvard University Press, 1968, 243. However, Marie Patricia McMahon in her dissertation, "The Quiet and Stability of this Free State: A New Look At the 'Independent Whigs,' John Trenchard and Thomas Gordon," argued that Trenchard and Gordon were not part of the other opposition writers. "They are," McMahon propounded, "first and foremost, radical-Whig theorists, deeply concerned for the safety and maintenance of the House of Hanover." See p. 209. Marie Patricia McMahon's dissertation. Washington D.C.: The American University, 1986.

43. *The Works of Tacitus* (London: Woodward and Peele, vol. I, 1728, and vol. II, 1731). (Dublin: Gunne, Smith and Bruce, vol. I in two parts, 1728, and vol. II in two parts, 1732). *The Works of Tacitus* (2 vols., London: Woodward and Peele, 1737). *Discours historiques, critques, et politiques sur Tacite* (2 vols., Amsterdam: F. Changuion,

1742). Translated by Pierre Daude. *Discours . . . sur Tacite* (2 vols., Amsterdam: F. Changuion, 1749). (3 vols., Amsterdam, 1751). *The Works of Tacitus* (5 vols., London: T. and T. Longman, 1753). (4 vols., London, 1757). *Discours . . . sur Tacite* (2 vols., Geneva: Cramer, 1759). Also translated by Pierre Daude.*Discous . . . sur Tacite* (Geneva: Cramer, 1762). *The Works of Tacitus* (5 vols., London, 1770). (5 vols., Dublin, 1778). *Discours . . . sur Tacite et sur Salluste* (3 vols., Paris: F. Buisson, 1794). A new edition by Pierre Daude. *The Works of Tacitus* (2 vols., London 1817). *The Reign of Tiberius Out of the First Six Annals* [of Tacitus] (London: W. Scott, 1886). A selection of part of the Gordon translation.

44. The Court was made up of the ministers and advisors to the King.

45. *Cato's Letters,* Number 15 "Of Freedom of Speech: That the same is inseparable from public liberty." Gordon authored this essay in the series.

46. *Discourses upon Tacitus*, "Of Freedom of Speech; and how reasonable it is."

47. *The Works of Sallust* (London: Woodward and Peele, 1744). (Dublin: John Smith, 1744). *Discours . . . sur Salluste* (2 vols., Geneva: Cramer, 1759). (2 vols., Geneva: Cramer, 1762). Translated by Pierre Daude. *The Works of Sallust* (London, 1762). (Glasgow: R. Urie, 1762). *Discours . . . sur Tacite et sur Salluste* (3 vols., Paris: F. Buisson, 1794). A new edition by Pierre Daude. *Discurso sobre los partidos y facciones . . . traducido de Ingles al Frances, y de este al Espanol* (Madrid, 1840). A translation of the first discourse on Sallust.

48. *The Works of Sallust*, Introduction.

49. Jacobson, *The English Libertarian Heritage*, xxx–xxxi.

50. David L. Jacobson, "Thomas Gordon's Works of Tacitus in Pre-Revolutionary America," *Bulletin of the New York Public Library* (New York: 1965) 69:62.

51. Gordon's *Tacitus* was reprinted, on the Continent, in at least five editions during the eighteenth century. *Discours historiques, critques, et politiques sur Tacite* (2 vols., Amsterdam: F. Changuion, 1742). Translated by Pierre Daude. *Discours . . . sur Tacite* (2 vols., Amsterdam: F. Changuion, 1749). (3 vols., Amsterdam, 1751). *Discours . . . sur Tacite* (2 vols., Geneva: Cramer, 1759). Also translated by Pierre Daude. *Discours . . . sur Salluste* (2 vols., Geneva: Cramer, 1759). (2 vols., Geneva: Cramer, 1762). Translated by Pierre Daude. *Discous . . . sur Tacite* (Geneva: Cramer, 1762). *Discours . . . sur Tacite et sur Salluste* (3 vols., Paris: F. Buisson, 1794). A new edition by Pierre Daude. *Discurso sobre los partidos y facciones . . . traducido de Ingles al Frances, y de este al Espanol* (Madrid, 1840). A translation of the first discourse on *Sallust*.

52. Jacobson, xxxii. See William H. Wickwar, *Baron D'Holbach, A Prelude to the French Revolution* (London: Allen and Unwin, 1935), pp. 74, 77, 241, 242.

53. *Brieven over de Vryheid en het Geluk des Volks onder pen Goede Regeerung in't Englesch uitgeegeven op den Naam van Cato* (3 vols., Amsterdam: Tongerlo, Houttayn, 1754). One hundred and thirty-three of *Cato's Letters* were translated into Dutch. *Dix-septieme lettre de Caton, traduite de l'Anglais de Thomas Gordon (Paris: A. Baudoin,* [1790]). Translated by J. L. Chalmel.

Chapter Two

Trenchard and Gordon's Works in the British North American Colonies

In order to evaluate the popularity of Trenchard and Gordon's works, one needs to estimate how available and accessible their works were in the colonies. It would be helpful to know how often their works appeared in libraries, newspapers, and what eighteenth-century colonists said about Trenchard and Gordon's works.

Eighteenth-century colonists could have been exposed to Trenchard and Gordon's works in several ways. Some read their works in book form, in pamphlets, or in newspapers and magazines. Most of Trenchard and Gordon's works that were in book form were brought from Europe, specifically from London. Two Philadelphia printers published the *Independent Whig* collection, once in 1724 and again in 1740.[1] Trenchard and Gordon's collection of essays titled *Cato's Letters* were not printed in their entirety in the colonies during the eighteenth century. Copies of the *Independent Whig* also arrived in the colonies from Europe along with Gordon's *Tacitus* and *Sallust*.

TRENCHARD AND GORDON'S WORKS IN LIBRARIES

Since books were expensive, people who read Trenchard and Gordon's works in book form probably borrowed them from libraries. There were several types of libraries in the eighteenth century including college or institutional, circulating, companies, and private.[2] A copy in a college or institutional library was almost certainly more widely read than a copy of the same work in a private library.

Evaluating the availability of Trenchard and Gordon's texts is one way of discovering how popular their works were in British North America. David Lundberg and Henry F. May did a fairly comprehensive study, which included catalogues from booksellers' auctions or sales and catalogues of the various types of libraries.[3] Most helpful for this thesis was their analysis of 92 libraries and their holdings from 1700 to 1776. Lundberg and May found Trenchard and Gordon's *Cato's Letters* collection, in book form, in 37% of the libraries catalogued. Relative to enlightenment works, *Cato's Letters* was one of the most popular texts to appear from 1700–1776. Works such as John Locke's *Essay Concerning Human Understanding* appeared in 41% of the libraries surveyed but Locke's *Treatise on Government* appeared only 15% of the time. Algernon Sidney's *Discourses Concerning Government* was present in 23% of the libraries. Only 7% of the libraries carried James Harrington's *Oceana* and even less popular was Thomas Hobbes's *Leviathan*, which appeared in 4% of the libraries.[4]

Trenchard and Gordon's *Cato's Letters* works should also be evaluated relative to contemporary political texts. From 1700–1776 *Cato's Letters* appeared just as often as the contemporary writer Joseph Addison's *Works*: both appearing in 37% of the libraries catalogued. Charles Louis de Secondat, Baron Montesquieu's *Spirit of Laws* and Alexander Pope's *Essay on Man* both appeared in 26% of the libraries studied. Henry St. John, Viscount Bolingbroke's works appeared considerably less than other political books. Bolingbroke's *Dissertation on Parties* was found in 5% of libraries, *The Idea of a Patriot King* in 10%, and his *Collected Works* appeared 12% of the time. Compared to other contemporary texts, *Cato's Letters* was very popular in eighteenth-century colonial America.[5] Unfortunately, the *Independent Whig*, Gordon's *Tacitus,* and *Sallust* were not part of Lundberg and May's study.

Since their study is an overall evaluation of libraries, it is worth investigating how popular and available Trenchard and Gordon's works were in different regions. Historian Trevor Colbourn published several lists of library holdings during the eighteenth century, including those of Harvard, Yale, The College of New Jersey, and Rhode Island College. He also published private library societies such as Redwood Library of Newport Rhode Island, New York Society Library, Library Company of Philadelphia, New Jersey Library Company, and the Charles-Town Library Society. In seven surviving lists from institutional and private libraries in Pennsylvania, New York, and New Jersey, Trenchard and Gordon's works were more popular than John Locke's. Six of the libraries had Trenchard and Gordon's *Cato's Letters* and Gordon's *Tacitus,* and five had the *Independent Whig,*[6] while only five of the libraries carried any one of Locke's works.

How does one know which of these books was borrowed, and how frequently? Two surviving loan-books from the Union Library of Hatboro in Pennsylvania (established 1755) suggests how many subscribers borrowed Trenchard and Gordon's works from 1762–1774.[7] Overall eight of the twenty subscribers borrowed one or more of Trenchard and Gordon's works. Four, including the only female subscriber Margret Rees, borrowed the *Cato's Letters* volumes. Three subscribers borrowed Trenchard and Gordon's *Independent Whig* series and one borrower signed out both the *Independent Whig* and *Cato's Letters*. In comparison, only four of John Locke's works circulated were borrowed but nine out of the twenty subscribers signed out one of Joseph Addison's texts. Other texts that were not political tracts but were popular with the subscribers were Robert Dodsley's *The Preceptor: Containing a General Course of Education* and Samuel Richardson's *Pamela*. Both were borrowed by seven subscribers, however *Pamela* was signed out several times by the same person, making *Pamela* the most frequently selected book of all.[8]

From this evidence, it appears that Trenchard and Gordon's works were quite popular among the library's subscribers compared to the other books in the Hatboro library. Most subscribers who signed out a couple of political texts included one of Trenchard and Gordon's works. One subscriber worthy of mention was Jacob Cadwalader who signed out all religious/history texts between 1763 and 1768 including Eusebus's three works, *Church History*, *Council of Trent, History of Popes*; Neels's *History of Puritans, Ecclesiastical History*; and Purvers *Bible*. Then in 1768, he signed out only *Cato's Letters*. Did Cadwalader all of a sudden become interested in Trenchard and Gordon? Or was his selection indicative of the political climate of the late 1760s? It might have been this latter factor that spurred his sudden interest in political rhetoric, but no one else rushed to borrow any of Trenchard and Gordon's works in the late 1760s and early 1770s from this library.

Library inventories of eighteenth-century southerners show a similar popularity of Trenchard and Gordon's works. But public lending libraries were generally more scarce in the south.[9] A catalogue list for the Charles-Town Library Society in South Carolina does exist and it indicates that by 1750 the library had the *Independent Whig* collection, *Cato's Letters*, and Gordon's *Tacitus*. Most of the lists of library inventories that exist were personal collections, which were lent out to family members and friends.[10] Historian Walter Edgar studied eighteenth-century libraries of South Carolinians. He listed books that were found five or more times in over a hundred and fifty personal libraries. Trenchard and Gordon's *Cato's Letters* appeared in nine of the libraries and their *Independent Whig* series seventeen times. Trenchard and Gordon's works were not nearly as popular as the *Spectator*, which was included in 77 of the libraries. John Locke's *An Essay Concerning Human Understanding* was included in thirteen of the inventories but *The Works of John Locke* were in only six. The *Works of Joseph Addison* were in fifteen of the library lists but Addison's (coauthored with Robert Steele) *Guardian* was in thirty-three of the inventories. Edgar's evidence does not place Trenchard and Gordon's works at the top a list of the most popular writings in South Carolina; but their works were impressively present.[11]

Historian Richard B. Davis in his work, the *Intellectual Life in the Colonial South 1585–1763*, gives further evidence of Trenchard and Gordon's popularity. Davis listed thirteen personal collections by southerners that included at least one work by Trenchard and/or Gordon. Five owned both the *Independent Whig* and *Cato's Letters*. Three possessed the *Cato's Letters* series only, two owned the *Independent Whig* collection solely, and four owned Gordon's *Tacitus*. Davis included library inventories from merchants, planters, lawyers, and clergymen to show the cross-class popularity of Trenchard and Gordon's works.[12]

TRENCHARD AND GORDON'S WORKS FOR SALE

Trenchard and Gordon's works appeared for sale by booksellers in several of the colonies. Two New England booksellers offered *Cato's Letters* and the *Independent Whig* for sale in 1772–1773.[13] A Philadelphia bookseller, David Hall, indicated in his Letterbook that he sold 19 copies of the *Cato's Letters* collection and 7 copies of the *Independent Whig* collection and Gordon's *Tacitus* from 1751–1769.[14] Another Philadelphia catalogue offered *Cato's Letters*, the *Independent Whig*, and Gordon's *Tacitus* for sale in 1760. A 1762 catalogue printed for New York and Pennsylvania inhabitants offered the *Independent Whig* and Gordon's *Tacitus*.[15]

Trenchard and Gordon's works were also offered for sale in newspapers. One or more of their works was offered for sale more than 80 times. Advertisements that offered the *Cato's Letters* collection appeared over 40 times in select newspapers during the century.[16] Newspaper advertisements listed the *Independent Whig* more than 35 times and Gordon's *Tacitus* more than 30 times.

Newspaper evidence shows that Trenchard and Gordon's works were offered for sale more often in Philadelphia than elsewhere in the British North America. The evidence suggests only that some of Trenchard and Gordon's works could easily have been obtained in the colonies, and from that one can infer that some copies were circulated. The actual number of copies circulated is impossible to determine from the available evidence. Trenchard and Gordon's works were available if one could afford to purchase them and wished to do so.

REPRINTING OF ESSAYS FROM THE *CATO'S LETTERS* COLLECTION IN EIGHTEENTH-CENTURY COLONIAL NEWSPAPERS[17]

Between 1721 and 1776, newspaper printers in the British North American colonies reprinted essays from Trenchard and Gordon's *Cato's Letters* collection on over 115 occasions.[18] Colonial printers only selected a little over fifty of the total 144 essays for reproduction in their newspapers. The majority of the essays reprinted in colonial newspapers discussed themes such as speech freedom, arbitrary vs. free governments, and human nature. The essays that colonial newspaper printers chose to republish do not reflect a representative sample of Trenchard and Gordon's themes. It is quite clear that the colonists had their own agenda and interests. For example, colonial printers only reprinted one of the essays that addressed corruption regarding government involvement with stock companies such as the South-Sea Company, which began as Cato's main focus.[19] The printers also did not reprint the essays that objected to monopolies or stock companies.[20]

Since colonists read only selections from Trenchard and Gordon's works, their understanding of these treatises developed in a distinctly colonial context. One must consider, though, that the meaning of what Cato represented depended on what most people read of *Cato's Letters*. One could try to figure this out, noting where Trenchard and Gordon's essays were reprinted and which ones were selected. In general, colonial newspaper printers selected essays on the preservation of liberty the most. The essays selected explained how to preserve liberty, which only existed in free governments where there were restraints put upon the people. Almost all the essays address liberty either directly or indirectly as the main reason for the essay.[21]

The colonial Cato believed that there was such a thing as human nature and that it was natural for humans to be selfish.[22] From Cato's perspective, therefore, people in power always tried to acquire as much power as possible by using any means necessary.[23] The word that was used in the eighteenth century to describe such dealings was corruption. A corrupt official was someone who made decisions and policies for particular groups in order to gain their support and acquire more power. The opposite of corrupt leaders were virtuous leaders. Virtue, in the eighteenth century, meant that a person acted in the best interest of the commonweal rather than just supporting measures to favor a particular group of people or interest.[24]

Trenchard and Gordon asserted that in order for free governments to exist, a virtuous populace and leadership must be maintained. Because they also alleged that most people would not act virtuously, Trenchard and Gordon claimed that people must make government ministers act in the best interest of the commonweal.[25] Trenchard and Gordon believed that the people that were out of power had not only a right but a *duty* to expose corrupt leaders and not support them.[26] The people needed to have a check over the actions of leaders and this made being virtuous in the best interest of the person in power because if a leader did not act virtuously, the people should expose him and he would eventually lose his power.[27] Hence, Trenchard and Gordon proclaimed the absolute necessity of freedom of speech and the press to expose corrupt people in power in order to maintain liberty in free governments.[28]

The freedom of speech and press, according to Trenchard and Gordon, were directly linked to creating and preserving free governments. Trenchard and Gordon, however, did not advocate an absolute freedom of speech. Instead, they affirmed that the freedom of speech pertained only to information that benefited the whole of society, which was information that exposed corruption.[29]

Between 1720 and 1760, printers published selections from *Cato's Letters* to address local controversies or debates. Colonists who reprinted essays from the Cato collection usually did so to bolster arguments against an alleged corrupt governor or powerful group involved in policy making. Trenchard and Gordon's essays in newspapers were used to encourage support from a particular group. The essays tended to be reprinted in whole, or in large sections and the printer usually acknowledged Trenchard and Gordon as the authors, especially early in the century.

The way the colonists used essays from Cato changed during the 1760s and 1770s. Colonial newspaper essay writers tended to borrow a few select phrases from Cato and then they couched these phrases within their own rhetoric. For example, in several essays of John Dickinson's *Letters from a Farmer in Pennsylvania,* he borrowed a few lines from several Cato essays.[30] Since Dickinson's collection went through several pamphlet editions and was reprinted in over nineteen colonial newspapers, the select sections from Trenchard and Gordon had a large distribution.[31]

Another example of how Cato essays were used by colonists differently from what had been their original intent; was the use of the two most popular essays titled "Of Freedom of Speech" and "The Right and Capacity of the People to Judge of Government." In the 1770s these essays were reprinted many times; however, only small sections were excerpted. Newspaper printers reprinted a few lines from essay Number 38 third hand, copying from a newly reprinted trial record in the case of John Peter Zenger that occurred in New York in the 1730s.[32] In 1770, a New York printer, John Holt, reprinted the trial defense that copied from *Cato's Letters* numbers 15 and 38. The newspaper printers of the *Pennsylvania Journal* and *New York Journal or General Advertiser* did not acknowledge that the ideas from the trial were those of Trenchard and Gordon. The printers either assumed that the readers knew, or they did not think recognition of the authors was necessary. They may not have known or cared where the ideas came from. Arguments in favor of freedom of speech and the right to judge government officials were now these of the Zenger trial, not Cato 15 and 38. This is evidence that eventually a few quotable lines from some of Trenchard and Gordon's works became part of the colonists' vocabulary.

During the immediate pre-Revolutionary period, colonists took a few popularized lines from a very few *Cato's Letters* essays and added their own examples to persuade the reader. The Cato of the 1720s-1750s represented something very different from the Cato that colonists thought of during the 1760s and 1770s.

The following section summarizes the most popular subjects that eighteenth-century colonial printers chose to reprint. The most popular essays in the colonies were the essays that discussed speech freedom and how it was necessary to preserve liberty. Out of the total 115 *Cato's Letters* essays reprinted in the colonies during the eighteenth century, 40 of them or 35% were about speech freedom. Essays that discussed freedom of speech were reprinted in newspapers in New York, Pennsylvania, Massachusetts, and South Carolina. The specific Cato essays on the subject of speech freedom that were reprinted included numbers 15, titled: "Of Freedom of Speech: That the same is inseparable from public liberty," Cato 38, "The Right and Capacity of the People to judge of Government," essay 32, "Reflections upon Libelling," and numbers 100 and 101 titled: "Discourses upon Libels."

Table 2.1 lists when and where number 15 "Of Freedom of Speech" was reprinted in the colonial newspapers.

Cato essay 15 began with the following statement: "Without freedom of thought, there can be no such thing as wisdom; and no such thing as public liberty, without freedom of speech...." Cato called freedom of speech "a sacred privilege" that was essential to "free" governments and a government could not be considered good unless people had freedom to speak. Cato also

Table 2.1. *Cato's Letters*, number 15 "Of Freedom of Speech" reprinted in colonial newspapers 1721–1775.

Newspaper	Date of Reprinting
New England Courant	2 July 1722
New York Weekly Journal	18 February 1733
American Weekly Mercury (AWM)	5 March 1733
New York Weekly Journal (NYWJ)	11 November 1734
South Carolina Gazette	5 June 1736
Pennsylvania Gazette	10 November 1737
Boston Evening Post	12 April 1742
South Carolina Gazette	9 July 1748
Independent Reflector (New York)	10 August 1753
Boston Gazette and Country Journal	21 April 1755
Pennsylvania Journal	23 February 1758
New York Journal or General Advertiser	19 March 1767
New York Journal or General Advertiser	19 November 1767
Boston Gazette and Country Journal	9 November 1767
Massachusetts Spy	28 March 1771
Massachusetts Spy	7 March 1771

warned readers that if someone wanted to take away liberty from citizens of a nation, he would begin by subduing the freedom of speech. Without the freedom of speech, Cato declared, the people could not defend their liberties.

Essay 15 drew upon antiquity to support the point about the importance of speech freedom. This essay included one of the most popular quotations taken from Trenchard and Gordon: "Freedom of speech is the great bulwark of liberty; they prosper and die together."[33] Cato ended his essay with the statement that the freedom of speech was of "such infinite importance to the preservation of liberty, every one who loves liberty ought to encourage freedom of speech."[34]

In correlation with number 15, essay 38 was reprinted at least 15 times in the colonies. "The Right and Capacity of the People to judge of Government" justified the need for speech freedom in a free country and usually was reprinted soon after or before the freedom of speech essay. Table 2.2 lists when and where number 38 was reprinted in colonial newspapers.

Cato 38 clearly emphasized the need for citizens to play an active role in government by keeping leaders honest. The essay ventured further than the argument that allowed people to judge government officials; the essay announced that it was a *duty* for men to judge government officials in order to keep officials in check. "It is the Duty of every individual," claimed Cato, "to be concerned for the whole, in which himself is included."[35]

Table 2.2. *Cato's Letters,* number 38 "The Right and Capacity of the People to judge of Government" reprinted in colonial newspapers 1721–1775.

Newspaper	Date of Reprinting
American Weekly Mercury (AWM)	13 February 1722
New York Weekly Journal (NYWJ)	10 December 1733
American Weekly Mercury (AWM)	20 September 1733
New York Weekly Journal (NYWJ)	21 July 1735
Pennsylvania Gazette	1 December 1737
Pennsylvania Gazette	10 November 1737
American Weekly Mercury (AWM)	27 April 1738
Pennsylvania Gazette	11 May 1738
South Carolina Gazette	1 August 1748
Independent Advertiser (Boston)	29 February 1748
Independent Reflector (New York)	21 December 1752
Boston Gazette and Country Journal	12 May 1755
Boston Gazette and Country Journal	19 May 1755
Pennsylvania Journal	15 March 1770 (from Zenger trial)
New York Journal or General Advertiser	29 March 1770 (from Zenger trial)
Pennsylvania Journal	26 March 1773
Pennsylvania Evening Post	28 March 1775
Pennsylvania Evening Post	30 March 1775

The essay sustained that anyone who disagreed that men should be involved in government was either "a tyrant or a slave." The essay also maintained that only when citizens involved themselves in government could it be considered free and just. In addition, a free government encouraged virtue and happiness, unlike tyrannical government, which encouraged corruption and unhappiness. The essay referred to ancient Rome as an example of when people were "happy" because the government was free. Then, after the "tyrannical government" of the Turkish Empire controlled the area, the people were starving and poor.[36]

Trenchard and Gordon claimed that because England had a Bill of Rights, which was enacted by parliament in 1689, people had a right to make their grievances known to the King or Parliament by petition.[37] The Bill of Rights, therefore, gave the power to judge government officials and policies to the people (represented by Parliament). Here, Cato asserted, lies the difference between people who live in free countries and those who were enslaved. In free countries, the government must consult and answer to the public, as opposed to "enslave[d]" countries where the private wills of the governors were "the sole end and motives of their administrations."[38]

In conclusion, after the discussion of speech freedom, several colonial printers published Cato 32, 100, or 101, which combined more explicitly speech freedom and the right to judge government officials. Cato confirmed that libels played an important role in society because they revealed the behavior of government officials. Because it was a "duty which every man owes to truth and his country" the means to judge government officials must be present.[39] The freedom of speech and writing, therefore, were necessary liberties. Without the liberty to speak against the government, people would not have the proper tools to carry out their responsibility to keep leaders in check. These essays further explained that it was better for a society to suffer from false libels than to deny the freedom of speech and press.

Colonial printers also found the Cato essays that discussed the nature of governments, arbitrary and free, very appealing. Numbers 35, 60, 61, and 62 directly discussed different types of governments. These essays were reprinted in newspapers in New York, Massachusetts, and Pennsylvania.

Essay 60 titled, "All Government proved to be instituted by Men, and only to intend the general Good of men," argued that government did not have any power except what man gave it and no just and free government could be framed without the consent of the people. The essay emphasized that the relationship between government officials and the people should be one of "mutual assistance."[40]

The essay continued with a discussion of the differences between arbitrary and free governments. Cato alleged that in a free government magistrates have their power qualified and "so divided into different channels, and committed to the direction of so many different men, with different interests and views, that the majority of them could seldom or never" agree to carry out injustice against the greater good of the people. In contrast, arbitrary governments were "where the rules of publick [sic] power were dictated by private and lawless lust. . . ."[41] The "secret" to free government, the essay proclaimed, was to make the interests of the governors the same as the interests of the governed. If the people supported only virtuous leaders who acted in the public's best interest, leaders would be forced to be virtuous public servants—not the other way around.[42]

Cato's Letters essay 62 discussed the "spirit and effects" of free and arbitrary governments. Liberty prevailed in free governments, according to Cato, and slavery resulted in arbitrary governments. Liberty, as defined by Cato, was "the power which every man has over his own actions, and his right to enjoy the fruit of his labor, art, and industry, as far as by it he hurts not the society, or any members of it."[43] Cato asserted that governments should only be concerned with the preservation of liberty because "where liberty is lost, life grows precarious, always miserable, often intolerable."[44] Cato contrasted this with a discussion of arbitrary governments that usually led to tyranny and political enslavement of the population. Cato defined slavery as living "at the mere mercy of another."[45]

Cato essay 35 discussed more differences between arbitrary countries and free countries. Public spirit, defined as the "love of one's country," in arbitrary countries was "to be blind slaves to the blind will of the Prince."[46] On the contrary, the author argued that public spirit was different in Protestant countries. Public spirit in free countries was to "reconcile the true interest of the governed and governors; it [was] to expose impostors, and to resist oppressors."[47] Public spirit in free countries, therefore, must be maintained by both leaders and citizens in order to preserve "liberty, plenty, ease, and security." Overall, the only way one could support one's country was to help preserve property, which according to the essay, was the only way to preserve national happiness. The author also propounded that whoever violated property was "an enemy to his country" and the public must punish him for his actions against the country.[48]

Colonial printers were also interested in the Cato essays that discussed human nature, and Cato essay 33 was one such tract. Essay 33 avowed that it was human nature for people to usurp as much power as possible. They believed that only God had power without control and that no one should be trusted with such power. When people were not held accountable for their actions, argued Cato, they always acted unaccountably. Any magistrate who was trusted with too much power, therefore, would always abuse it. Furthermore, Cato averred that "if every man had his will, all men would exercise dominion, and no man would suffer it."[49] The essay stated that rulers must be enclosed within strict confines or else they would take and do as they wanted. Since men do not naturally submit to laws, Cato wrote, government was necessary, and he defined government as "the mutual contract of a number of men, agreeing upon certain terms of union and society, and putting themselves under penalties, if they violated these terms, which were called laws. . . ."[50] The essay advocated the idea that selfishness was an essential part of human nature and "we can scarce be too much upon our guard against each other."[51] Essays 40 and 42 also discussed the nature of humans and mans "selfish spirit" and they were reprinted on several occasions.

Cato's Letters essay 96 discussed the human propensity to divide into factions or parties. In Cato essay 96, the authors argued that the differences between Whig and Tory were slight because of the nature of the parties in the eighteenth century. The essay asserted that the original principles of the Tory party were to "let the crown do what it pleased."[52] The principles of the Whig party were to not let the crown act without the consent of the people. Cato claimed that "A Tory under oppression, or out of a place, is a Whig; a Whig with power to oppress, is a Tory."[53] The essay stated that "all men dread the power of oppression out of their own hands, and almost all men wish it irresistible when it is there." Furthermore, "parties like or dislike our constitution, just as they are out of power, or in it," propounded Cato.[54]

Cato continued to reveal the author's view on human nature. The essay maintained that "nothing [was] more wild, fickle, and giddy, than the nature of man . . . . We swallow greedily today what we loathed yesterday, and will loathe again tomorrow." Furthermore, the essay claimed that the nature of men was "selfish and prone to error."[55]

The essay ended with a call for people of the nation to set aside their "party" allegiances, since they really did not mean anything. The authors advocated that people consider what was best for the whole of the nation instead of what was good for one party. Moreover, the people needed to establish rules to govern that would prevent oppression from any party and this could be "done by restraining the hands of power, and fixing it within certain bounds as to its limits and expense."[56]

Cato essays 37 and 115 both addressed the subject of power and how that related to government officials. Newspapers in New York, Pennsylvania, Massachusetts and South Carolina all printed at least one of the essays. Essay 37 was directly quoted from Algernon Sidney and was titled "Character of a good and of an evil Magistrate." Simply stated: "the good magistrate seeks the good of the people" and the evil magistrate was one that believed the people were made for him.[57] Good magistrates "uphold the rightful power of a just magistracy, encourage virtue and justice" while ill magistrates are corrupt and "always open the way for him by vitiating the people, corrupting their manners, destroying the validity of oaths. . . ."[58]

Essay 115 titled: "The Encroaching Nature of Power, ever to be watched and checked" gave specific characteristics of "good" and "bad" magistrates. The essay asserted that a "good" leader must look out for the welfare of "the people" and not for their personal interests. A good magistrate must believe that he was made for the people and not believe that the people were made for him. A good leader was also one who carried out justice and was virtuous. Bad magistrates, described Cato, were men who were out only for personal gain and used their power against the people. The essay also implored the people of a nation to judge the leader for his actions and held that it was the duty of the people to support good magistrates and reject bad magistrates.

Two Cato essays that appeared in colonial newspapers, numbers 34 and 131, addressed the subject of flattery and reverence. Essay number 34 defined flattery as a "pernicious weed, which grows and prevails everywhere," but mostly exists in the court.[59] The essay argued that servants, in fear of not receiving favors, had a proclivity for telling falsehoods to superiors. In that regard, flattery destroyed leaders in the past because many leaders ended up having a false sense of power. Cato then described several examples of how flattery ruined people. Cato's examples included several stories from antiquity and the story of how Henry III of France fell victim to his alleged flatterers.[60]

Cato 131, "Of Reverence true and false," declared that one must respect only people who were good leaders, and not honor men who were not. One must be careful not to revere tyrants, stated the essay, because if one did, slavery resulted. The essay counseled that men might be "great" and powerful but if they were unjust, they should not be revered. Satan, the essay asked, had a lot of power; should people worship him? The essay cautioned that honoring people because they had a good name or held an office was dangerous to free societies and people needed to expose all corrupt officials. Because one exposed a corrupt official, however, this did not mean that the office the man held should be dishonored. The essay affirmed that if a person in power "acts ridiculously or knavishly in it, do I dishonor that office by condemning or exposing the man who dishonors it?"[61]

A few colonial printers also found Cato's several essays on religion interesting enough to reprint. Printers in Pennsylvania and New York reprinted *Cato's Letters* 123, 124, 128, and 130. Cato defined religious enthusiasm as "a flaming conceit that we have great personal interest with the deity."[62] Cato continued to argue that religious enthusiasts were dangerous to society because they based their beliefs on irrational premises. Cato also criticized people who followed corrupt clergy. Cato essay number 128 assured that "priestcraft and tyranny" were "inseparable . . . and proved by the priests to be *jure divino* ["by divine law"]."[63] Cato described the hierarchy in the Anglican church as corrupt and explained how its policies often violated "public liberty." Cato claimed that the leaders of the Church used people like slaves and that humans had the ability to stop the injustices done to them by the Church.[64]

As the above section indicates, colonial printers were very selective about what they borrowed from Trenchard and Gordon's *Cato's Letters* collection. Colonial printers did not choose to reprint a representative sample of Trenchard and Gordon's ideas. Colonists reprinted essays to encourage popular participation in politics. Colonists found essays on speech freedom and the right to judge government officials most appropriate to reprint in newspapers because of the political culture of these areas. This filtering of Trenchard and Gordon's works through the printers had an impact on what some people thought Trenchard and Gordon stood for, if they read only a select few of their works in newspapers, especially in colonies where people learned about *Cato's Letters* from newspapers.

REPRINTING OF ESSAYS FROM THE *INDEPENDENT WHIG* SERIES IN EIGHTEENTH-CENTURY COLONIAL NEWSPAPERS

Colonial printers reprinted only a few of Trenchard and Gordon's essays from the *Independent Whig* series in eighteenth-century newspapers. The *New England Courant* was the first newspaper to reprint an essay from the *Independent Whig* collection in the British North American colonies. In the 28 August-4 September 1725 issue, *Independent Whig* essay Number IX titled: "Of the Clearness of Scripture," was reprinted. The essay explained God's law and how His law was given exactly and specifically to the people. The essay then gave a lesson from the Bible including the story of the Covenant God made with Abraham.[65]

Selections from the *Independent Whig* were also reprinted in a couple of colonial newspapers in New York. A New York magazine,[66] the *Independent Reflector*,[67] borrowed sections from the Trenchard and Gordon's *Independent Whig* collection on at least four occasions. The sections taken from the *Independent Whig* emphasized again the corrupt nature of human beings. More specifically, however, the essays from the *Whig* collections addressed the corrupt nature of the Catholic Church. The essays selected from the *Independent Whig* series usually warned that Church leadership was often dangerous to free societies.

The essays postulated that the clergy were men and all men had the capability of being corrupt. Moreover, clergymen were considered more dangerous than most people in power because people revered them simply because of their position in the church and not because of their behavior.[68]

REPRINTING OF SECTIONS FROM GORDON'S *DISCOURSES UPON TACITUS*

Sections of Gordon's introduction to his translation of *Tacitus*, titled *Discourses upon Tacitus*, were also reprinted in a few colonial newspapers in the eighteenth century. Most of the printers reprinted only a paragraph or two in their papers. In the *New York Weekly Journal* a paragraph was reprinted on 19 November 1733. The quote stated : "Where no liberty is allowed to speak of Governors, besides that of praising them, their praises will be little believed; their tenderness and aversion to have their conduct examines will be apt to prompt people to think their conduct guilty or weak. . . ."[69] Also in 1733, a New York newspaper called the *New York Gazette* described Gordon's *Discourses upon Tacitus* as being founded "upon truth, and the reason of things."[70] The *New York Mercury* on 3 March 1755 also reprinted a few paragraphs from Gordon's *Discourses Upon Tacitus*. The selection made reference to the reasons why Rome fell, which was because of the corrupt leaders, especially Caesar.

Two colonial newspapers reprinted sections from Gordon's *Discourses upon Tacitus* during the 1770s. The *Boston Gazette* on 1 April 1771 reprinted three long paragraphs from Gordon's work. The passage listed Switzerland as a country that had overcome its tyrannical leaders. The selection explained how corrupt government officials had suppressed the population in Switzerland to the point that the people resisted. The selection stated: "the oppression, the acts of violence were general, constant, deliberate and increasing." The essay alleged that it was human nature to acquire as much power as possible. The selection warned that the people must watch over the leaders to ensure they do not acquire too much power.[71]

The last known reprint of Gordon's *Discourses* in the British North American colonies in the eighteenth century occurred on 24 April 1776 in the *Pennsylvania Gazette*. The quote stated that "Monarchy, according to Plato, is the best government or the worst. . . ."[72] The *Gazette* reprinted only a small selection from Gordon's work.

POSSIBLE READERSHIP OF TRENCHARD AND GORDON'S WORKS

It is obvious that some eighteenth-century colonists read Trenchard and Gordon's works. One needs to be more specific, however, about how many people could have read their works and who had the opportunity to do so. As examined, people read Trenchard and Gordon's works if they bought their texts, borrowed them from private libraries or friends, or read newspapers that reprinted some of their works.

It is nearly impossible to figure out how many people read Trenchard and Gordon's works in book form. As evidence suggests, some colonists did own one or more of Trenchard and Gordon's works as per surviving library catalogues. More people had access to newspapers than to books in the eighteenth century. If people read some of Trenchard and Gordon's works, it was probably their material that was printed in local newspapers and this needs to be evaluated before the importance of Trenchard and Gordon's works can be explained.

Estimates indicate that about 5% of white families in the colonies in 1765 received a newspaper weekly.[73] The figure was derived by taking the estimated white male population, able to bear arms,[74] in the colonies in 1765 and dividing that by about 14,000 weekly newspapers circulated in that same year. This estimate does not mean that only 14,000 people read a newspaper every week. This number should probably be multiplied by at least five because most newspapers were read by several people.[75]

Newspapers tended to be passed from one person to the next so several people could have read the papers in taverns or coffeehouses. There were also people who occasionally read newspapers, which is very difficult to calculate into the equation. From this extrapolation, however, approximately 14% of the white population most likely read a weekly newspaper before 1760.

Newspaper readership, however, was not distributed evenly throughout the colonies. The colonial newspapers that reprinted Trenchard and Gordon's works the most were located in New York City, Philadelphia, and Boston. Newspapers in South Carolina, Virginia, and Maryland reprinted very few of their works if at all before 1760. Moreover, people living in the backcountry did not have easy access to Trenchard and Gordon's works that were reprinted in newspapers.[76] Some areas, such as Delaware, East and West New Jersey, Rhode Island, and Maryland had access to newspapers from New York, Philadelphia, or Boston.

Pennsylvania newspapers reprinted more of Trenchard and Gordon's works than any other colonial newspaper during the eighteenth century. For example, from 1720 to 1734 about 25 *Cato's Letters* essays were reprinted in newspapers and about 800 copies of each newspaper were printed. Given an estimated white population of 45,000, and stipulating that each issue reached an estimated five individuals, the percentage of whites in Pennsylvania who read a newspaper with an essay from Trenchard and Gordon reached nearly 10%.

Trenchard and Gordon's works were also reprinted in New York colonial newspapers. The total white population over the age of sixteen was about 31,400 in 1749.[77] The newspaper that reprinted the largest number of Trenchard and Gordon's works was the *New York Weekly Journal*. This weekly journal probably printed between 600–1000 copies per week.[78] If one estimates that five people read one paper then the total number of people being able to read one issue of the *New York Weekly Journal* was from 3000 to 5000 people. This would mean 10–15% of the New York population could have read an issue of the *New York Weekly Journal*.

In other colonies such as Massachusetts, the percentage of people who could have read Trenchard and Gordon's works in newspapers was about the same. Colonial printers in Massachusetts reprinted many of Trenchard and Gordon's works. An estimation of the population in Massachusetts in 1721 was about 94,000. According to population records, this number should be divided by 4 to indicate the number of white males over the age of 16. This would make the estimated white adult males in Massachusetts in 1721: 23,500. In this year the newspaper that reprinted several of Trenchard and Gordon's essays was the *New England Courant*. Approximately six hundred issues of the *Courant* were printed per week. Taking into consideration that five people read one issue, about 3000 people could have read an issue with Trenchard and Gordon's essays reprinted. This would equal about 13% of the white adult male population in Massachusetts who might have read one of Trenchard and Gordon's essays.

For South Carolina the percentage of adult white males who had access to a newspaper was far greater because the white population was a lot smaller in the colony than in northern colonies. The total white adult males between the ages of 16–60 was about 5,000 in 1750.[79] The *South Carolina Gazette* probably printed about 600 copies of an issue and five people most likely read one copy making the readership about 3000. If these calculations are accurate, it could be that 60% of the white adult males in South Carolina read a few essays from Trenchard and Gordon that were reprinted in the *Gazette*.

In contrast, in Virginia before 1760, the *Virginia Gazette* never reprinted one of Trenchard and Gordon's essays, which makes the readership zero in that colony's newspapers. This was also the case in Maryland, Georgia, and North Carolina. A few essays, however, did appear after 1760, which means a large percentage of adult white males had access to some of Trenchard and Gordon's ideas in southern newspapers in the latter part of the century.

This readership information allows us to draw some tentative conclusions. One such assumption is that Trenchard and Gordon's works were more widely read in New York, Pennsylvania, and Massachusetts newspapers than in other colonies before 1760. About 10–15% of the white male adult population could have read their essays in select newspapers. This leads us to infer that people who read Trenchard and Gordon's work in newspapers had a different understanding of their ideas than those who read their books, since only a select few were reprinted.

Since southern newspapers did not reprint Trenchard and Gordon's essays nearly as often; only the *South Carolina Gazette* reprinted four of *Cato's Letters* before 1760. In the south, people who knew about Trenchard and Gordon's works probably read their works in book form. This meant that a more comprehensive form of Trenchard and Gordon's ideas existed in the South than in colonies further north where the newspapers educated people on their ideas.

Because people in Massachusetts, New York, and Pennsylvania were exposed to a filtered Trenchard and Gordon message, it is important to flesh out what exactly was taken from Trenchard and Gordon. It is also imperative to know how the essays were used, why they were selected, and what these select essays meant to the reading public before 1760 and then how different their role was after 1760. This will be the task of the next several chapters.

NOTES

1. In 1724 S. Keimer and in 1740 Andrew Bradford. No known records exist that indicate how many copies were printed or how many were sold. Library lists that have survived and had a copy of the *Independent Whig* did not indicate Keimer or Bradford as the printer or where or when the work was published.

2. David Lundberg and Henry F. May, "The Enlightened Reader in America," *American Quarterly* Volume 28, Issue 2 (Summer, 1976), 262–293.

3. Lundberg and May, "The Enlightened Reader in America," 262–293.

4. Lundberg and May, "The Enlightened Reader in America," 262–293.

5. Lundberg and May, "The Enlightened Reader in America," 262–293.

6. Trevor Colbourn, *The Lamp of Experience: Whig History and the Intellectual Origins of the American Revolution* (Indianapolis, IN: Liberty Fund, 1965), 245–274.

7. Chester T. Hallenbeck, "A Colonial Reading List," *The Pennsylvania Magazine Of History and Biography* Vol. 61, No. 4 (1932), 289–341.

8. Hallenbeck, "A Colonial Reading List," 289–341.

9. Richard Beale Davis, *Intellectual Life in the Colonial South 1585–1763* (Knoxville, TN: The University of Tennessee Press, 1978), 526.

10. Davis, *Intellectual Life in the Colonial South 1585–1763*, 526.

11. Walther B. Edgar, "The Libraries of Colonial South Carolina" (Doctoral dissertation, University of South Carolina, 1969).

12. Personal libraries of southerners who had one or more of Trenchard and Gordon's works: Arthur Miller of Kent County, Maryland had a copy of the *Independent Whig*; William Carmichael of Chestertown, MD had the *Independent Whig*; Robert King Carter of Corotoman, Virginia had a copy of Gordon's *Tacitus* in 1732; Robert Carter Councillor of Nomini Hall, VA had a copy of Trenchard's Tracts (could have been *Cato's Letters* or the *Independent Whig*) and Gordon's *Tacitus*; Thomas Jefferson of Monticello, Virginia had acquired a copy of Gordon's *Tacitus* and *Sallust* between

1770 and 1815; Jefferson also indicated that by 1783 his library included *Cato's Letters* and the *Independent Whig* collections; Daniel Parks Custis of New Kent County, VA had a copy of *Cato's Letters* and the *Independent Whig*; Eleazer Allen of North Carolina had both of Trenchard and Gordon's works; Joseph Vail of New Bern, NC had a copy of *Cato's Letters*; Planter John Mackenzie of Charleston, South Carolina had a copy of *Cato's Letters* and Gordon's *Tacitus* by 1772; Edward Flower, merchant, had copies of *Cato's Letters* and *Independent Whig*; Thomas Gadsden of Charleston, SC had both Trenchard and Gordon's works; Thomas Burrington of Savannah, Georgia had Trenchard and Gordon's works (not specifically indicated).

13. Colbourn, *The Lamp of Experience*, 275–277. Henry Knox in a 1773 Catalogue offered *Cato's Letters*, *Independent Whig*, and something titled Trenchard and Gordon's *Tracts* 2V. Smit and Coit, two Hartford Booksellers in a 1772 advertisement offered *Cato's Letters* and the *Independent Whig*.

14. Colbourn, *The Lamp of Experience*, 279–282.

15. Colbourn, *The Lamp of Experience*, 283. Colbourn did not find any of Trenchard and Gordon's works for sale in the Southern colonies. He found Dixon and Hunter's catalogue of books for sale of Williamsburg, Virginia in 1775, an advertisement William Aikman made in 1774–1775. Colbourn also looked at lists of books from bookseller George Wood of Charleston, and booksellers Nicholas Langford, Francis Nicholson, Robert Wells, Samuel Gifford of Charleston and found none of Trenchard and Gordon's works for sale.

16. See Appendix 1.

17. See Appendix 2.

18. This number indicates essays from the *Cato's Letters* series that were reprinted in their entirety or more than 2/3rds of the essay. This does not include appearances of a few lines or paragraphs from one of their Cato essays.

19. *Cato's Letters*, Number 10.

20. Did not reprint the essays that attacked stockjobbers and financiers, which included *Cato's Letters* Numbers 2–7, 9, 10, 12, 21, 21, 22, 29,58, 87–91, 107.

21. *Cato's Letters*, Numbers 33, 35, 38, 59, 50, 62, 115. These essays addressed liberty and free governments directly.

22. *Cato's Letters*, Numbers 31 and 40.

23. *Cato's Letters*, Number 33.

24. Landsman, *From Colonials to Provincials*, 155 and Pocock, *Machiavellian Moment. Cato's Letters*, Numbers 14, 15, 26, 27, 37, 40, 45, 56.

25. *Cato's Letters*, Number 16.

26. *Cato's Letters*, Numbers 27, 32, 35, 38, 131.

27. *Cato's Letters*, Numbers 59 and 60.

28. *Cato's Letters*, Numbers 15, 32, 38, and 100.

29. *Cato's Letters*, Number 100.

30. See Chapter 5.

31. Carl F. Kaestle, "The Public Reaction to John Dickinson's Farmer's Letters," *Proceedings of the American Antiquarian Society* 78, pt. 2 (1969): 323–353.

32. The John Peter Zenger trial is explained further in Part II. The lawyer defending John Peter Zenger, Andrew Hamilton, used *Cato's Letters* Number 15 and Num-

ber 38 to argue for this client. The titles were Of Freedom of Speech: That the same is inseparable from public Liberty and The Right and Capacity of the People to judge of Government. The trial record was printed by Zenger in 1736 under the titled: *A Brief Narrative of the Case and Trial of John Peter Zenger Printer of the New York Weekly Journal for a Libel*. Then John Holt of New York reprinted the *Narrative* in 1770. Consequently, colonial newspapers had not reprinted from Cato's Number 38 since 1755 and then immediately after the reprinting of the Zenger trial narrative in 1770 the *Pennsylvania Journal* and the *New York Journal or General Advertiser* reprinted the selections from the trial that came from Cato Number 38.

33. This phrase was found more than twenty times in colonial newspapers.
34. *Cato's Letters*, Number 15. 4 February 1720. "Of Freedom of Speech; That the same is inseparable from public Liberty."
35. *Cato's Letters*, Number 38 "The Right and Capacity of the People to judge of Government."
36. *Cato's Letters*, Number 15.
37. According to the Bill of Rights, the Parliament had the right to petition the king.
38. *Cato's Letters*, Number 38.
39. Quotation was specifically from *Cato's Letters* Number 32, which appeared in *The New England Courant* (Boston) on 4 September 1721, the *New York Weekly Journal* on 25 February 1734, and the *New York Gazette* on 2 April 1770.
40. *Cato's Letters*, Number 60 "All Government proved to be instituted by Men, and only to intend the general Good of men."
41. *Cato's Letters*, Number 60.
42. *Cato's Letters*, Number 60.
43. *Cato's Letters*, Number 62 "An Enquiry into the Nature and Extent of Liberty; with its Loveliness and Advantages, and the vile Effects of Slavery."
44. *Cato's Letters*, Number 62.
45. *Cato's Letters*, Number 62.
46. *Cato's Letters*, Number 35 "Of Public Spirit."
47. *Cato's Letters*, Number 35.
48. *Cato's Letters*, Number 35.
49. *Cato's Letters*, Number 33 "Cautions against the natural Encroachment of power."
50. *Cato's Letters*, Number 33.
51. *Cato's Letters*, Number 33.
52. *Cato's Letters*, Number 96 "Of Parties in England; how they vary, and interchange Characters, just as they are in Power, or out of it, yet still keep their former Names."
53. *Cato's Letters*, Number 96.
54. *Cato's Letters*, Number 96.
55. *Cato's Letters*, Number 96.
56. *Cato's Letters*, Number 96.
57. *Cato's Letters*, Number 37 "Character of a good and of an evil Magistrate, quoted from Algernon Sidney, Esq." Algernon Sidney was a popular hero in the late seventeenth century and throughout the eighteenth century. He was famous for his

controversial doctrines on government. During the Exclusion crisis, Sidney and other leading Whigs tried to exclude the Catholic heir to the throne, James Duke of York. Their efforts failed; therefore, Sidney and others planned to revolt. Before the revolt occurred, Sidney was arrested and charged with treason. He was found guilty and executed on 7 December 1683. See Algernon Sidney's *Discourses Concerning Government* edited by Thomas G. West. (Indianapolis, Indiana: Liberty Fund), 1996.

58. *Cato's Letters,* Number 37.
59. Trenchard and Gordon considered the "Court" to be the people in power.
60. *Cato's Letters,* Numbers 34 and 131.
61. *Cato's Letters,* Number 131 "Of Reverence true and false."
62. *Cato's Letters,* Numbers 123, 124, 128 and 130.
63. *Cato's Letters,* Numbers 123, 124, 128 and 130.
64. *Cato's Letters,* Numbers 123, 124, 128 and 130.
65. *New England Courant,* 28 August-4 September 1725.
66. An eighteenth-century magazine usually appeared monthly and the contents of the essays were usually instructive. Essays about morality, scientific discoveries or experiments, poetry, fiction, riddles, and some foreign and domestic news. See Frank Luther Mott, *A History of American Magazine 1741–1780* (Cambridge: Harvard University Press, 1957).
67. The periodical was named in part after Trenchard and Gordon's *Independent Whig* collection.
68. The *Independent Reflector* borrowed selections from Trenchard and Gordon's *Independent Whig* series on at least five occasions. On 22 March 1753, *Independent Whig* Number V. 19 July 1753, *Independent Whig* III. 27 September 1753 *Independent Whig* XLIX. 18 October 1753 *Independent Whig* XXVII.

There was a short-lived periodical in Boston, Massachusetts called: *The Censor* that reprinted *Independent Whig* essay number XXVIII on 7 March 1772. However, the essay in *The Censor* was not from the *Independent Whig* series and was not part of the *Cato's Letters* collection. The essay was on the subject of libels, which sounded like it was one of Trenchard and Gordon's essay, but it is not a direct match.

69. *New York Weekly Journal,* 19 November 1733.
70. *New York Gazette,* 28 January-4 February 1733. Number 432. Page 3 col. 1.
71. *Boston Gazette,* 1 April 1771. Number 834. Page 3, col. 1–2.
72. *Pennsylvania Gazette* 24 April 1776. The article also said: "the testimony of another professed Whig, nay an *Independent Whig* (the famous Gordon, in his *discourse upon Tacitus*) shall come next."
73. Mott, *American Journalism,* 59. This study's possible readership limits the scope to white males. Further research is needed to determine if women or free blacks read newspapers articles involving politics.
74. The ability to bear arms indicates the male had approached adulthood as defined in the eighteenth century.
75. Mott, *American Journalism,* 59.
76. There were no newspapers in the backcountry in the eighteenth century.
77. Wells, 112. The population in the colony of New York in 1749 was 73,348. One would be led to believe that the non-white inhabitants probably did not read the

newspapers, therefore, if one minuses 14.4% for the non-white population the total is 62,785.9. Then, take one half of that because about half of the population was under sixteen and probably not reading the newspapers. The total white people over the age of sixteen in New York in 1749 could have been about 31,393.

78. According to Isaiah Thomas the necessary minimum of copies that needed to be printed in order to pay for the print was 600 copies. Thomas also estimated that most papers printed between 600–1000. Benjamin Franklin with his press, however, produced more copies—between 1500–2000 copies per week.

79. Evarts B. Greene and Virginia D. Harrington, *American Population Before the Federal Census of 1790* (New York: Columbia University Press, 1932), 175.

Part II

Chapter Three

Trenchard and Gordon's Works in Massachusetts Newspapers Before 1760

A Boston newspaper was the first paper to reprint selections from *Cato's Letters* in British America. Trenchard and Gordon's works were subsequently reprinted on several more occasions throughout the eighteenth century. Since the political culture in Boston and much of Massachusetts was based on popular politics, the reprinting of Trenchard and Gordon's works fit well into Boston society. Their essays, however, made a prominent appearance only in short-lived opposition newspapers before 1760. In 1720, opposition to the Puritan church's control over society led to the reprinting of eight different essays. In 1748, a controversy between the Governor of Massachusetts, William Shirley, and an opposing faction spurred on the reprinting of eight Trenchard and Gordon essays. Another controversy in 1755 revolving around a more extensive excise tax caused a heated press debate. The exchange of discourse led to the republishing of several of Trenchard and Gordon's essays, especially on the subject of freedom of speech and the right to judge government officials.

The appearance of Trenchard and Gordon's essays in Massachusetts newspapers supports Richard Bushman's findings in his book, *King and People in Provincial Massachusetts*. Bushman aimed to reconstruct the political culture in provincial Massachusetts and found that the two most important words were "the people" and "the king." The word "people," according to Bushman, had power "to invest politicians with moral authority."[1] Bushman concludes that the opposition parties were not republicans hostile to monarchical government. Trenchard and Gordon had a very similar philosophy underlying their works; they advocated balanced government and believed that the people must keep government institutions virtuous.[2]

The first colonial newspaper to reprint selections from Trenchard and Gordon's *Cato's Letters* series was the *New England Courant*. The printing of Cato's political essays marked a stark contrast to the prior subject of publications in other Boston newspapers. Unlike these other papers, the *Courant* included little news and few advertisements; instead the paper printed political essays.[3] Puritan culture encouraged printing and writing; however, only Puritan publications were approved by the colonial officials.[4]

The *New England Courant* was established in 1720 as a protest newspaper against the Governor, Samuel Shute, and several leading members of the Puritan Church in Boston. The printer, John Checkley, dedicated most issues to essays that opposed Puritan leader Cotton Mather. One of the key opposition points was Mather's project to inoculate people for smallpox. Checkley used the inoculation issue as a platform for protesting against Puritan authority. He argued that the Puritan clergy could not be trusted and that the citizens of Boston must protect themselves against the church officials.

In 1721, James Franklin took over the *New England Courant*. After Franklin was put in jail for seditious libel, his brother, Benjamin Franklin, took over the paper. As printer, Benjamin Franklin chose to reprint several essays from *Cato's Letters* and he also wrote essays under the pseudonym "Silence Dogood," which quoted heavily from Trenchard and Gordon's essays.[5] There were seven essays from the *Cato's Letters* series and two from the *Independent Whig*. The Trenchard and Gordon essays that were reprinted in the *Courant* discussed speech freedom, human nature, honor, and religion.

Several essays discussed the importance of freedom of speech. Essay Number 32 explained the difference between true and false libels. True libels were an asset to society because they informed the public of corrupt government officials. False libels were not an asset, yet, would always exist. This essay seems to have been directed to the Puritan leadership that considered a libel a very serious crime. Puritans believed that speech was a powerful tool and was often dangerous if used improperly.[6] The essay admitted that a libel was still a libel even if the information was true. One, therefore, did not have the right to print against a person's "private or personal failings." If a person's crime, however, affects the public then the crime should be made known. The essay also claimed that to expose "wickedness" was a "duty which every man owes to truth and his country" and should be considered positive in free societies.[7]

On the same subject, Benjamin Franklin, under the pseudonym Silence Dogood, reprinted part of *Cato's Letters* Number 15. Franklin reprinted the essay in response to the imprisonment of his brother James for printing material with which the government of Massachusetts did not agree. The witty

Benjamin Franklin was able to get away with reprinting the essay not only because he used a pseudonym but also because he declared that the essay was an "abstract from the *London Journal*" and was not "anything of my own."[8] By doing this, Franklin embraced the colonial power structure then gave authority to the metropolitan center by using British authors.

The essay began with the popular opening: "without freedom of thought, there can be no such thing as wisdom; and no such thing as public liberty, without freedom of speech; which is the right of every man. . . ."[9] The essay qualified the "right" by the addition of the statement that every man has this right as long as he did not "hurt" another man unjustly.

The essay declared that freedom of speech was a "sacred privilege" that was so fundamental to free governments that the protection of property and the freedom of speech always belonged together. Further, Cato avowed that "in those wretched countries where a man cannot call his tongue his own, he can scarce call anything else his own."[10] Consequently, the essay warned that if someone tried to restrict freedom of speech, he should be considered a traitor to the country.

Other subjects discussed while the *Courant*'s supporters opposed the established government were human nature and corruption. Trenchard and Gordon's essay numbers 27, 31, 33, and 57 were reprinted.[11] These select essays indicated that because of human nature, corruption was widespread. Number 27 explained that corruption destroys liberty in society. Virtue, therefore, must be encouraged by all. Furthermore, a selection from essay 31 contended that the people must judge government officials on all their actions and support only people who act virtuously. This essay defined virtuous government officials as ones who made decisions that benefited the entire society, not just a part or a group of people.[12]

The *Courant* also published several essays that discussed honor and flattery. Honor, as explained in essay 57, is when someone does well for others and is honest. People should be honored only if they display such characteristics. Essay 34 was reprinted, which discussed the problems that occurred when someone was honored or flattered for not doing well for society. Flattery, as defined by Trenchard and Gordon, was the act of lying to a superior just to win favors from him. Flatterers agreed with anything that their superiors said even if the flatterer thought the idea or action was wrong. The essay stated that flattery was "a poisonous and pernicious weed, which grows and prevails every where."[13] Flattery, according to Cato, was "a vice which has finally ruined many nations, and many princes, and one time or other hurt all."[14] This essay on flattery considered it a duty for men to honestly evaluate their superiors, which supported the idea that men should be actively involved in local affairs.[15]

Essay 33 discussed human nature and how it affects government. Cato affirmed that it was human nature for men to desire to increase their power; therefore, a man's power must be limited. The essay further explained that everyone was entitled to liberty; however, government was needed to protect the liberty of a nation. Government, the essay propounded, "was the mutual contract of a number of men agreeing upon certain terms of union and society, and putting themselves under penalties, if they violated these terms, which were called laws."[16] Puritan New Englanders believed that citizens of a community mutually agreed to live in the community and abide by the rules of the town. The essay concluded that "power, without control, appertains to God alone, and no man ought to be trusted with what no man is equal to."[17]

Sections from the *Independent Whig* numbers IX and X, reprinted in the *Courant*, emphasized the importance of the covenant between God and man.[18] The essay attacked the role of the priest in the Church. "A learned and virtuous layman," the essay assured, "can instruct more effectively, and pray more devoutly and successfully than an ignorant and profane Priest."[19] The essay concluded with similar sentiment and declared that men should take part in religion and not allow the established Church to dictate to the people.

The *Boston News Letter*[20] also chose to reprint a Trenchard and Gordon essay that discussed religion during the 1720s but did not include essays on the freedom of speech as the *Courant* did numerous times. The printer of the *Boston News Letter*, Bartholomew Green, began his printing business in Boston in 1690. In April of 1704, he began publishing the *Boston News Letter*, which was the first newspaper printed in British North America. Green was known for his piety and benevolence and was a highly respected member of the Puritan Boston community.[21] Green, therefore, would have little use for reprinting opposition literature like Trenchard and Gordon's works. The newspaper had very little political rhetoric throughout the 1720s. Green, however, found one essay directed against the Roman Catholic Church that would have supported his Puritan view.[22]

On 5–12 March 1724 the printer included *Cato's Letters* 128 titled an "Address to such of the Laity as are Followers of the disaffected clergy." Cato asserted that people must be wary of the clergy and their teachings. The essay addressed the unjust treatment the Anglican Church committed against the Puritans. Furthermore, Cato argued that the "priestcraft and tyranny [were] ever inseparable, and go hand-in-hand infinite other oppressions were brought upon the poor people."[23] The essay supported this by the use of specific examples from the past. The essay continued to claim that the Church constantly misled the people and abused its power. "Popery is the most dreadful machine," Cato argued.[24]

The *Boston Evening Post* was another Boston newspaper that reprinted a couple of Trenchard and Gordon's essays but was not an opposition newspaper. The printer of the *Boston Evening Post*,[25] Thomas Fleet, reprinted two of Trenchard and Gordon's *Cato's Letters* in 1742. He opened a printing shop and printed books and pamphlets until 1731 when he started the *Weekly Rehearsal*,[26] which Fleet changed to the *Boston Evening Post* in 1735. The *Weekly Rehearsal* and the *Boston Evening Post* were meant to contain essays on moral, political, and commercial issues.[27]

Fleet borrowed most of his essays on moral, political, and commercial issues from various British newspapers, Bolingbroke's serial set the *Craftsman*, and the serial collection called *The Reflector*.[28] Fleet, however, chose to reprint two of Trenchard and Gordon's essays in order to justify his role as an informer of the people.[29] He printed Cato essays Numbers 15 and 100; both discussed freedom of speech.[30]

The *Independent Advertiser* reprinted several of Trenchard and Gordon's essays in 1748. Samuel Adams and several of his friends in response to controversial policies of the Governor of Massachusetts, William Shirley, created this short-lived opposition newspaper. Governor Shirley served fifteen years beginning in 1741 and ending in 1756. According to historian John A. Schutz, Shirley's term brought "an era of relative good feeling."[31] In 1748, however, a controversy broke out between Shirley and several prominent citizens.

Tensions were high in the colony of Massachusetts from 1747 through 1749. Some people in the colony were unhappy with Shirley's war policies and the declining economy due to inflation. The *Independent Advertiser* was created to oppose the administration's policies. The official printers were Daniel Fowle and Gamaliel Rogers, but most of the controversial essays and articles were written by leading anti-administration citizens such as Samuel Adams and William Douglass. The opponents of Shirley attacked the administration because they believed that the government had encouraged materialism that was increasing in the colony. Because of this the *Independent Advertiser* also attacked wealthy merchants and minor officials who were supporters of the allegedly materialistic administration.[32]

The essays that appeared in the *Independent Advertiser* discussed several subjects such as human nature, corruption, how to keep a free government, and why a free government was more beneficial than an arbitrary government. The editor of the *Independent Advertiser* printed several essays from the *Cato's Letters* series that discussed human nature. Cato number 43 explained that human nature compelled people to strive to be superior to others. Cato claimed that "no man would choose to have any man his equal, if he could place himself above all men."[33] That was why people were not equal in society, even though everyone was born equal.[34]

Then, by using *Cato's Letters* 26, the group opposed to the administration protested against the allegedly corrupt government officials. The essay addressed the issue of corruption and how it had an ill effect on society. "Liberty cannot be preserved," Cato proclaimed, "if the manners of the people are corrupted."[35]

Cato stated that government officials should be supported only if they were virtuous. The people, Cato averred, must require leaders to act in the best interest of the people. Once leaders were held accountable for their actions and understood that society would support them only if they were virtuous, then government and society would be free and just. Cato also argued that government leaders must not be concerned with "riches." Cato referred to ancient Sparta where material wealth did not make one popular or powerful. Only virtuous actions made someone a respected citizen.[36]

Cato expanded this notion and explained how a corrupt governor valued vanity, luxury, and riches over serving the public good. Many opponents of the administration believed that Governor Shirley was this type of leader. Consequently, less than a month after this essay was printed several leading citizens, namely Joseph Heath, James Allen, and John Tyng, attempted to cut Shirley's salary.[37]

Cato's Letters 38 explained that since it was human nature to be corrupt, the people must take part in keeping government officials in check. Cato announced that "honesty, diligence, and plain sense" were the only talents necessary to be a "good" leader. Government should not be a trade and people should not prosper off of the spoils of government. Cato believed that farmers were great leaders because of their simple way of life.[38] The ideas in this essay exemplified the beliefs of Samuel Adams and his friends.[39]

The essay also addressed the need for public truth to be displayed when it came to the actions of government officials. Every man, Cato professed, "ought to know what it concerns to know" and government concerns every citizen. The essay concluded that all private men had a duty to check government officials because the liberty of all in society was at stake.[40]

Since it was the duty of the people to judge government officials, the *Independent Advertiser* reprinted an essay that explained what a "good" leader did as opposed to an "evil" leader.[41] This particular essay was probably selected because of the May elections taking place in the House. The introduction to the essay illuminated the author's reason for submitting the Cato essay entitled the "Character of a Good and of an Evil Magistrate, quoted from Algernon Sidney, Esq."[42] The essay explained the difference between "good" and "evil" leaders. The good magistrate, the essay claimed, "seeks the good of the people" and he also carries out justice. The good ruler will act in the interest of the people before he acts in his own. The essay also explained how the ruler and the people had a mutual relationship in a "good" government. The good ruler will act in the best interest of the people and in return the people will reward him by supporting his leadership.[43]

On the other hand, the essay demonstrated what an "evil" leader does to the country. Sidney explained that "when a magistrate fancies he is not made *for the people*, but the people *for him*; that he does not govern *for them*, but *for himself* . . ."[44] the magistrate is "evil." The essay continued to claim that a country that was ruled by an evil ruler would "certainly divide the nation into parties." Moreover, the essay asserted that people were not happy living under a magistrate who did not consult the public welfare before making decisions.[45] This essay fit very well into the environment of the May elections of the House. The outcome of the May elections did not dramatically alter the House or affect the Council; however, the election did harden the opposition to the administration.[46]

Further discussion of government and leaders appeared in the *Independent Advertiser* when *Cato's Letters* 35 on the subject of public spirit was reprinted. Cato defined public spirit as "the love of one's country." Cato propounded that not many people really know what it means to love one's country. The essay claimed that in arbitrary countries, public spirit meant the people must be "blind slaves to the blind will of the Prince."[47] Supposedly in Protestant countries or free countries, however, public spirit meant all people would "reconcile the true interest of the Governed and Governor, it is to expose impostors and to resist oppressors, it is to maintain the people's liberty, plenty, ease, and security."[48]

The essay further castigated government officials who acquired wealth at the public's expense. This part of the essay also fit very well into the controversy taking place in Massachusetts at this time. Cato claimed that when government officials had arbitrary power, the leaders always had too much and the people too little. The essay warned the reader about the dangers of governments that were arbitrary.[49]

One of the last Trenchard and Gordon essays to appear in the *Independent Advertiser* discussed the benefits of living in a government free from arbitrary control. The essay titled the "Arts and Sciences the Effects of Civil Liberty only, and ever destroyed or oppressed by Tyranny" explained how free societies encouraged industry and arbitrary governments squelched trade. Cato explained that "where there [was] liberty, there are encouragements to labor, because people labor for themselves; and no one can take from them the acquisitions which they make by their labor."[50] On the other hand, Cato held that in tyrannical governments, "where life and property, and all things must depend upon the humor of a Prince, the caprice of a minister . . . few people can have money and they that have must lock it up, or bury it to keep it."[51]

Cato concluded that a country and society prospered much more in a free country than in a country that had an arbitrary government. The essay advocated that trade was an important measure of a country's wealth and trade was more successful in a free country. Cato propounded that "in free countries, men bring out their money for their use, pleasure, and profit, and think of all ways to employ it for their interest and advantage."[52]

In 1754, the colony of Massachusetts was in the middle of a controversy over a more extensive excise tax. A pamphlet war broke out between the supporters of the tax and people against the new tax. During the initial protest, printers published essays from Bolingbroke's *The Craftsman* collections to support their opposition against the excise tax. In 1755, however, after the controversy reached the Board and Trade, the editors of the *Boston Gazette*, Benjamin Edes and John Gill, chose to reprint six essays from Trenchard and Gordon.[53] The third issue of the *Gazette* reprinted *Cato's Letters* Number 15 on the subject of the freedom of speech.[54] The other popular essay chosen in 1755 was Cato essay Number 38 on the subject of citizens having the right, and moreover the duty, to judge government officials.[55]

On 19 May 1755, Edes and Gills chose to reprint an uncommon Cato essay entitled: "Of the natural honesty of the people, and their reasonable demands. How important it is to every Government to consult their Affections and Interests."[56] Cato argued in this essay that all men possess "common sense" and "sound judgment" and that was why men should create governments. Cato explained that "when plain honesty and common sense alone governed the public affairs, and the morals of men were not corrupted with riches and luxury," public liberty was best preserved.[57]

Cato continued to argue that the first principles of power were in the people and that people in power must be forced to refer to the people. Furthermore, government officials could either rule "by the sword" or "must be maintained by consent."[58] Cato declared that in free countries people in power had to preserve the affections of the people or be forced out.

In Boston, Trenchard and Gordon's works were mostly reprinted in short-lived opposition newspapers before 1760. Bostonians used opposition newspapers to enter into political debates and controversies. This use of *Cato's Letters* before 1760 gave Bostonians important lessons on how to oppose unpopular actions implemented by government officials.

NOTES

1. Richard L. Bushman, *King and People in Provincial Massachusetts* (Chapel Hill, NC: The University of North Carolina Press, 1985), 4.

2. Bushman, *King and People*, 4.
3. Isaiah Thomas, *The History of Printing in America* (New York: Weathervane Books, 1970), 111.
4. Thomas, *The History of Printing in America*, 199–200.
5. Wm. David Sloan and Julie Hedgepeth Williams, *The Early American Press, 1690–1783* (Westport, CT: Greenwood Press, 1994), 23–30.
6. See Jane Kamensky's essay "Words, Witches, and Women Trouble: Witchcraft, Disorderly Speech, and Gender Boundaries in Puritan New England." *Essex Institute Historical Collection*, 128,(1992) 228–307. Kamensky explains how the Puritans saw "disorderly" speech as a serious crime because the Puritans believed speech was a powerful weapon if used improperly. She argued that in seventeenth-century New England, "the proposition that words were capable of inflicting real damage would not have aroused debate. The ruling elite and common folk alike recognized that speech was a source of power and of danger, and that the boundaries between speaking and doing were fuzzy ones."
7. *New England Courant*, 4–11 September 1721. *Cato's Letters*, Number 32. The entire essay was not reprinted in the *Courant*, however, it appears that the printer had planned to but never did. At the end of the 4–11 September issue was a note that the rest would appear in the next paper, however, it did not.
8. *New England Courant*, 4–11 September 1721.
9. *New England Courant*, 2–9 July 1721. *Cato's Letters*, Number 15.
10. *New England Courant*, 2–9 July 1721.
11. The following selections were reprinted in the *New England Courant*: *Cato's Letters*, Number 27 was reprinted on 30 April 1722, Number 31 was reprinted on 16 July 1722, Number 33 on 16 October 1721 and continued on 23 October 1721, Number 57 was summarized on 2 April 1722.
12. *New England Courant*, 30 April 1722. *Cato's Letters*, Number 27 and on 16 July 1722 *Cato's Letters*, Number 31.
13. *New England Courant*, 2–9 October 1721. *Cato's Letters*, Number 34.
14. *New England Courant*, 2–9 October 1721. *Cato's Letters*, Number 34.
15. *New England Courant*, 2–9 October 1721. *Cato's Letters*, Number 34.
16. *New England Courant*, 23–30 October 1721. *Cato's Letters*, Number 33.
17. *New England Courant*, 23–30 October 1721. *Cato's Letters*, Number 33.
18. The use of the term "Covenant" a between man and God would probably not have aroused disapproval from the Puritan leaders since the entire existence of their life was to fulfill the Covenant.
19. *New England Courant*, 28 August- 4 September 1725. *Independent Whig* IX and X.
20. The *Boston News Letter* changed names to the *Boston Weekly News Letter* then changed names again to the *Massachusetts Gazette*.
21. Thomas, *The History of Printing in America*, 89–92.
22. Green probably reprinted this essay from the *American Weekly Mercury* of Philadelphia because this same essay, Number 128, appeared in the *Mercury* on 4–11 February 1724. This is a good possibility since Bradford had sent his *Mercury* all over the colonies because he had free shipping because of his postmaster position at this time.

23. *Boston News Letter*, 5–12 March 1724. *Cato's Letters*, Number 128.

24. *Boston News Letter,* 5–12 March 1724. No. 1050. *Cato's Letters* Number 128. *Boston News Letter* 7 July 1748. The issue quoted Trenchard and Gordon: "Men are so conceited that they think they deserve every thing they want or think they want, and may do every thing to procure it."

25. The *Weekly Rehearsal* preceded the *Boston Evening Post*, both printed by Thomas Fleet. Apparently, Fleet intended to have the *Boston Evening Post* be a continuation of the *Weekly Rehearsal*. The last issue of the *Rehearsal* was number 201 and the first issue of the Boston Evening Post was number 202. However the second issue of the Post was numbered 2. Trenchard and Gordon's works failed to appear in the *Weekly Rehearsal*. The only reference to Cato was a Latin phrase taken from the Roman Cato, which appeared on 1 May 1732.

26. *The Weekly Rehearsal* was first printed by John Draper but edited by Fleet. However, in April of 1733 Fleet took over as the printer.

27. Thomas, *The History of Printing in America*, 100.

28. Essays from *The Craftsman* were reprinted on 12 May 1738, 29 May 1738, 12 February 1739, 25 February 1740, 9 June 1740, 16 June 1740, 27 October 1740, 1 December 1740, 9 January 1749. Essays from the *Reflector* were reprinted on 28 January 1751, 4 February 1751, 11 February 1751, 25 February 1751, 3 June 1751, 10 June 1751, 17 June 1751, 24 June 1751, 15 July 1751, 19 August 1751, 13 July 1752, 17 August 1752, 18 December 1752, 1 January 1753, 8 January 1753, 6 August 1753, 20 August 1753. From the *Spectator*, Fleet reprinted an essay on 15 September 1755.

29. Evidence suggests that Fleet reprinted the essays from a bound published edition of the *Cato's Letters* collection because he noted that Number 15 was reprinted from Volume I page 96.

30. *Boston Evening Post*, *Cato's Letters,* Number 15 was reprinted on 12 April 1742 and *Cato's Letters,* Number 100 was reprinted on 17 May 1742.

31. John A. Schutz. *William Shirley: King's Governor of Massachusetts* (Chapel Hill: The University of North Carolina Press, 1961), 137.

32. Benjamin W. Labaree, *Colonial Massachusetts: A History* (New York: KTO Press, 1979).

33. *Cato's Letters*, Number 43 was reprinted in the *Independent Advertiser* on 22 August 1748.

34. *Cato's Letters*, Number 45 was reprinted in the *Independent Advertiser* on 11 January 1748.

35. *Independent Advertiser*, 13 June 1748. *Cato's Letters,* Number 26.

36. *Independent Advertiser*, 13 June 1748. *Cato's Letters*, Number 26.

37. Schutz, *William Shirley,* 137.

38. *The Independent Advertiser*, 29 February 1748. *Cato's Letters*, Number 38.

39. William M. Fowler, Jr. *Samuel Adams: Radical Puritan* (New York: Longman, 1997).

40. *Independent Advertiser*, 29 February 1748. *Cato's Letters,* Number 38.

41. *Cato's Letters*, Number 37 reprinted in the *Independent Advertiser* on 16 May 1748.

42. *Independent Advertiser*, 16 May 1748. The introduction stated that "the ill consequences which attend an abuse of power are so many, that we cannot wonder at the universal murmurs, which it occasions, I shall not now attempt to point at any particular instances of this nature among us, as it may be done to much better purpose in a Nomination of Officers, which its whispered is shortly intended; the Sentiments and descriptions of the following extract may therefore not be unreasonable, and if it needed any Commendation, it might receive a sufficient one from the approved Character of its author, who thought and wrote as well as any Man in the Age wherein he lived, and at last fell a sacrifice to tyranny. . . ." The "author" is Algernon Sidney. *Cato's Letters* essay Number 37 is a direct quote from one of Algernon Sidney's works.

43. *Independent Advertiser*, 16 May 1748. *Cato's Letters*, Number 37.

44. Emphasis added by the contributing author to the *Independent Advertiser*.

45. *Independent Advertiser*, 23 May 1748 Number 21. *Cato's Letters*, Number 37.

46. Schutz, *William Shirley*, 137.

47. *The Independent Advertiser*, 25 January 1748. Number 4. *Cato's Letters*, Number 35.

48. *The Independent Advertiser*, 25 January 1748. Number 4. *Cato's Letters*, Number 35.

49. *The Independent Advertiser*, 25 January 1748. Number 4. *Cato's Letters*, Number 35.

50. *Independent Advertiser*, 26 June 1749. Number 78. *Cato's Letters*, Number 67.

51. *Independent Advertiser*, 26 June 1749. Number 78. *Cato's Letters*, Number 67.

52. *Independent Advertiser*, 26 June 1749 Number 78. *Cato's Letters*, Number 67.

53. See Paul S. Boyer's essay "Borrowed Rhetoric: The Massachusetts Excise Controversy of 1754." *WMQ*, Third Series, Volume 21, Issue 3 (July, 1964), 328–351.

54. *Boston Gazette and Country Journal*, 21 April 1755. *Cato's Letters*, Number 15.

55. *Boston Gazette and Country Journal*, 21 April 1755 *Cato's Letters*, Number 15. And on 12 May 1755 *Cato's Letters*, Number 38.

56. *Boston Gazette and Country Journal*, 23 June 1755 *Cato's Letters*, Number 24.

57. *Boston Gazette and Country Journal*, 23 June 1755 *Cato's Letters*, Number 24.

58. *Boston Gazette and Country Journal*, 23 June 1755 *Cato's Letters*, Number 24.

Chapter Four

Trenchard and Gordon's Works in New York Newspapers Before 1760

The politics of eighteenth-century New York revolved around factions that constantly jockeyed for power and position.[1] The factious nature of the political culture in the colony of New York created a welcoming environment for opposition political rhetoric.[2] New Yorkers began reprinting selections from *Cato's Letters* and the *Independent Whig* as early as the 1730s; however, New York printers only selected a few of these essays, which led to a different understanding of the political philosophy underlying Trenchard and Gordon's works.

Context is imperative when delineating Trenchard and Gordon's significance. New Yorkers selectively exploited their works during three highly politicized controversies in the eighteenth-century. First, a select few of their *Cato's Letters* essays appeared in the 1730s during a controversy between Governor William Cosby and a group of opponents. Second, a few essays from *Cato's Letters* and the *Independent Whig* series, appeared in the 1750s during a dispute over the creation of King's College (now Columbia). Finally, a very few excerpts materialized during the 1760s when the conflict between England and the colonies began. In all three cases, Trenchard and Gordon's works were used within a context of oppositional politics, further developing a connection between popular protests against imperial policy and the colonists' selective use of *Cato's Letters* and the *Independent Whig*.

John Trenchard and Thomas Gordon's works made a flamboyant entrance into the New York political scene in the 1730s. Specifically, Trenchard and Gordon's essays signed "Cato" landed in the middle of a battle for power in New York. Even though only sixteen complete Cato essays appeared in the *New York Weekly Journal (NYWJ)*, Cato became the subject of over twenty-five issues of the *NYWJ* and the opposing newspaper, the *New York Gazette (NYG)*.

The controversy that brought about the use of *Cato's Letters* began with the arrival of a new New York governor in August of 1732, Sir William Cosby. Before arriving in the colony, Cosby had a reputation for being arrogant and greedy, and he was known for his insatiable appetite for power. The appointment of Cosby troubled many New Yorkers since the governor was the King's representative and possessed considerable authority. Governors could "veto legislation, dissolve or prorogue the Assembly, appoint officials, establish a court of chancery, grant land titles, and distribute military supply contracts."[3] Therefore, the New York elite either needed to gain Cosby's favor or they would find themselves losing out on the spoils of government.

The former governor, Montgomerie, died in 1731 and the senior member of the Council, Rip Van Dam, took over as acting governor until Cosby traveled from London to New York. Upon his arrival, Cosby determined that because it was an unusual custom for the senior member of the Council to take over as governor, Rip Van Dam should give up one half of his salary to Cosby. Rip Van Dam refused and Cosby decided to take him to court. Cosby made matters worse when he decided to bypass the usual court proceeding, which involved a jury, and instead asked the New York Supreme Court to set up a proceeding without a jury, an equity court. Cosby thought he would have a better chance of winning his money in such a venue because judges decided equity court decisions and they usually favored the plaintiff. Cosby's actions infuriated some of the New York elite including the Chief Justice of the Supreme Court, Lewis Morris.[4]

On April 9, 1733, Chief Justice Lewis Morris denied Cosby's request for an equity court. In response to Morris's decision, Cosby accused Morris of being a drunkard and not fulfilling his duties properly as chief justice. Morris in turn published his decision to deny Cosby an equity court and circulated it to the people of New York in defense of his judgment. Cosby then decided to suspend Morris from his duties as chief justice and gave the position to James DeLancey, a known opponent of Lewis Morris.[5]

The lines had been drawn; Cosby and several leading New York families including the DeLancey's, were in one camp and Morris and his supporters were in the other. Both groups took their campaigns to the press. Realizing they "must play the game of tavern politics" to gain support, the Morris faction hired printer John Peter Zenger to create a newspaper, the *New York Weekly Journal*, in order to voice their opinion.[6] The DeLancey/Cosby faction used the well-established *New York Gazette* to counter the opposition. These newspapers brought the controversy to the attention of New Yorkers and other residents of British America. What began as a battle to keep or take power within a small elite group developed into an inter-colonial affair.

Prior to the 1730s, the only New York newspaper was the *New York Gazette,* which William Bradford founded in 1725.[7] Bradford was the official printer for the government, which meant he received a substantial amount of money from the government to run his printer shop. It was, therefore, unnecessary to popularize the paper in order to gain more subscriptions. Bradford was content with printing foreign and domestic news in his newspaper and anything that the government wished to print. The *Gazette* sufficed until the discord surrounding Governor Cosby. In response to the controversy, the Morrisite faction hired its own printer, John Peter Zenger, to print the *New York Weekly Journal (NYWJ)*, which served as its voice in the political dispute. Zenger, a German immigrant, began his printing career as William Bradford's apprentice, and then he opened his own printing shop. Zenger struggled and barely made a living with his printing shop until the Morrisite faction hired him to print the *New York Weekly Journal.* Essentially, Zenger did not author most of the articles in the *NYWJ.* Instead, Lewis Morris, James Alexander, and William Smith, Sr. wrote the majority of the articles.[8]

James Alexander was the primary contributor to the *NYWJ.* It has been suggested that the newspaper was his idea. Alexander already had published several articles in Bradford's *Gazette* when it was the sole newspaper in New York City. Governor Cosby had also showed distaste for Alexander.[9]

Trenchard and Gordon's essays fit well into the controversy between Governor Cosby and the Morrisites. Over twenty issues of the *New York Weekly Journal* from 1733 to 1751 consisted of essays from Trenchard and Gordon's collection. One of the first essays printed elaborated on the importance of press freedom. The Morrisite faction probably initiated its newspaper with this declaration for good reason. It attempted to persuade readers that the newspaper's main objective was to represent "truth" and liberty, not to serve as a faction group to oppose the governor.

Zenger's newspaper published essays by Trenchard and Gordon that depicted an optimistic view of the role of "the people" in government and these essays encouraged New York citizens to become politically involved. *Cato's Letters* 15, 38, and 131 were reprinted, which addressed the freedom of speech, the right to judge government officials, and the necessity for people to expose corruption in government.[10] Because the people must keep a check on government officials, Cato's essays asserted, the freedoms of speech and press were essential to carry out that duty. Furthermore, Cato believed that the "freedom of speech [was] the great bulwark of liberty; they prosper and die together; and it [was] the terror of traitors and oppressors and a barrier against them—it produce[d] excellent writers and encourage[d] men of fine genius."[11]

The first essay attributed to Cato, but not written by Cato, was published in the *New York Weekly Journal* on 12 November 1733.[12] The front page of the

NYWJ argued that the liberty of the press was a necessary part of a "free" government.[13] The essay alleged that it was better to have some false reports than to have no news at all. Furthermore, it was the responsibility of the reader to question printed information and not to believe everything in print. The press's main role, the essay declared, was to draw the people's attention to certain subject matters. In conclusion, the essay argued that without the freedom of press, the people might suffer "under the tyranny of an insolent, rapacious, infamous minister."[14]

On 19 November 1733 the issue continued with a similar theme and quoted from Gordon's *Tacitus*: "Where no liberty is allowed to speak of Governors, besides that of praising them, their praises will be little believed; their tenderness and aversion to have their conduct examined, will be apt to prompt people to think their conduct guilty or weak . . ."[15]

The first authentic Trenchard and Gordon essay reprinted in Zenger's *NYWJ* was titled "The Right and capacity of the people to judge of government."[16] The subject of the essay furthered the idea that press freedom was important in free societies. The essay clearly emphasized the need for citizens to play an active role in government. This essay encouraged popular politics and also established the role of the press in helping people play a part in government affairs. Citizens must publish information about corrupt activities done by officials that negatively affected the public welfare in order to keep government officials honest. The essay ventured further than the argument that allowed people the right to judge government officials; the essay asserted that it was a *duty* for men to judge government officials in order to keep ministers in check. "It is the Duty of every individual," claimed Cato, "to be concerned for the whole, in which himself is included."[17]

The essay claimed that anyone who disagreed that men should be involved in government was either "a tyrant or a slave." The essay also maintained that only when citizens involved themselves in government could the government be considered "free" and "just." In addition, a free government encouraged virtue and happiness unlike tyrannical government, which led to corruption and unhappiness. The essay referred to ancient Rome as an example of when people were "happy" because the government was free. Then, after the "tyrannical government" of the Turkish Empire controlled the area, the people were starving and poor.[18]

On 31 December 1733, the *New York Weekly Journal* reprinted another controversial essay from *Cato's Letters* entitled "Of Reverence true and false."[19] The essay declared that one must respect only men who were good leaders and not honor men who were not. One must be careful, warned the essay, not to revere tyrants because if one did, slavery resulted. The essay counseled that men might be "great" and powerful but if they were unjust, they should not be revered. The essay cautioned that honoring people because they had a good name or held an office was dangerous to free societies and people needed to expose all corrupt officials. This essay implied that people have the capability to know who was a good leader and who was not. Hence, the essay, when used in this context, encouraged the populace to involve themselves in government affairs.

In response to the *NYWJ*, a letter appeared in William Bradford's *Gazette* that protested Zenger's reproduction of Trenchard and Gordon's works.[20] The author wrote that Zenger's reprinting of the Trenchard and Gordon essay was taken out of context. He stated: "I could not but regret to see one of the greatest names in antiquity prostituted to a plagiary." The essay described how the author decided to reread Gordon's *Discourses upon Tacitus*, which preceded Gordon's translation of *Tacitus*. The author of the letter said that after he consulted Gordon's *Discourses* he found that Zenger had "artificially" put together the works of Trenchard and Gordon and used the essays improperly. The *NYWJ*, however, reprinted primarily from Trenchard and Gordon's collection signed Cato, not Gordon's *Discourses*.[21] Gordon's *Discourses* addressed similar subjects as *Cato's Letters;* however, the rhetoric was not nearly as earnest in Gordon's text.[22] It is unknown why the author of the letter chose to read Gordon's *Discourses upon Tacitus* and not *Cato's Letters*. The rhetoric in Gordon's *Discourses* was less emotional and less passionate in prose; however, the arguments were, for the most part, consistent with the essays that comprise *Cato's Letters*.

The respondent continued to argue that Zenger's use of Trenchard and Gordon's works promoted factions and propagated sedition, and that was not an objective of Trenchard and Gordon's works. He explained that the words of Cato and Gordon's *Discourses* were "swollen into a gigantic size and have undergone an alteration by Peter Zenger's types at New York."[23] He maintained that Gordon's *Discourses* were founded "upon truth, and the reason of things"; however, because Zenger "dismembered and [had] taken to pieces" his work, Zenger used Trenchard and Gordon to spread untruths. Dryden concluded that Zenger committed libel and should be punished by the revocation of his printing privileges.[24]

The Morris faction quickly responded to the *Gazette's* accusations. A letter in the *NYWJ* asked Dryden why he read Gordon's *Discourses* and not *Cato's Letters*, since the essays were taken directly from *Cato's Letters*. The response continued to explain that the essays were not "tacked together" to tell untruths. The essays, for the most part, claimed the respondent, were reprinted word for word.[25]

In response to the articles reprinted by the *NYWJ*, Governor Cosby accused the newspaper of libel and requested that the New York Grand Jury hear a case against Zenger.²⁶ The court refused to hear the case at that time. In response the next issue of the *NYWJ* reprinted Trenchard and Gordon's essay titled the "Of Freedom of Speech." The essay declared that the freedom of thought or speech was an "essential element to free governments."²⁷

The essay forewarned that anyone who attempted to take the liberty away from the people of a nation usually began by the revocation of the freedom of speech. Because the people must keep a check on government officials, Cato's essay asserted that the freedom of speech and press were essential since it was the only way to carry out that duty. Furthermore, Cato believed that the "freedom of speech [was] the great bulwark of liberty; they prosper and die together; and it [was] the terror of traitors and oppressors and a barrier against them it produce[d] excellent writers and encourage[d] men of fine genius."²⁸

Bradford chose to reprint parts of Joseph Addison and Robert Steele's *Spectator* series to answer Zenger's reprint of Trenchard and Gordon's essay of the freedom of speech. Bradford reprinted Addison's *Spectator* number 451 because it discussed issues that explained the dangers of spreading lies and scandals. Consequently, Bradford argued that the freedom of speech that Trenchard and Gordon wrote about did not include spreading lies.²⁹

Zenger's *NYWJ* responded to the *New York Gazette* article possibly, to continue threatening the Governor to sue Zenger for libel with the republication of the essay titled "Reflections upon Libeling."³⁰ This essay supported the idea that people ought to expose corrupt government officials and called it a "duty which every man owes to truth and his country," and that this could never be considered a libel. Cato admitted that there would always be libels if writing and printing existed; however, they believed it was better to have many libels than to restrict or stop the freedom of the press.³¹

Zenger used this opportunity to discuss the nature of human beings, which furthered the argument in favor of exposing corrupt government officials.³² The essay avowed that it was human nature for people to usurp as much power as possible. They believed that only God had power without control and that no one should be trusted with such power. When people were held unaccountable for their actions, argued Cato, they always acted unaccountably. Therefore, any magistrate who was trusted with too much power would always abuse it. Furthermore, Cato believed that "if every man had his will, all men would exercise dominion, and no man would suffer it."³³ The essay contended that rulers must be enclosed within strict confines or else they would take and do as they wanted. Since men do not naturally submit to laws, Cato wrote; government was necessary and defined as "the mutual contract of a number of men, agreeing upon certain terms of union and society, and putting themselves under penalties, if they violated these terms, which were called laws. . . ."[34] The essay advocated the idea that selfishness was an essential part of human nature and "we can scarce be too much upon our guard against each other."[35]

In response to the above essay, a letter signed Peter Scheme in the *New York Gazette* again criticized Zenger's *NYWJ*. Peter Scheme sarcastically wrote that since the last accusations against the *NYWJ*, at least "scurrility and ribaldry takes not up above eight or ten lines of his last paper."[36] He called Zenger's republication of *Cato's Letters* his "winter-nights-entertainment of questions and command, and printing over again his law-quibble-catechism."[37] In conclusion, Scheme's letter asserted that Zenger's essays were romanticizing Cato and created several romantic characters referred to as "so many American Cato's."[38]

Seemingly undisturbed by the response, the *NYWJ* reprinted two sections of two different essays titled "Of the Restraints which ought to be laid upon public rulers" and "the encroaching nature of power, even to be watched and checked."[39] The essay stated that nothing but "fear and selfish consideration can keep men within any reasonable bounds" and in the absence of fear people step outside of their proper confines as far as possible. Furthermore, there were two potential enemies of a country, one foreign and possibly the other a country's own leader. The essay also argued that a country's worst enemy was its own leader because he usually stole "from the people in degrees." In order to guard against the encroachment of power by a magistrate, maintained Cato, leaders must be checked and "confined within certain bounds."[40]

In the *New York Gazette* an anonymous writer responded to Zenger's newspaper. The unnamed author of the letter said that Trenchard and Gordon's argument that the liberty of the press was essential to "free" governments did not apply to Zenger's *Journal* because of the misuse of Trenchard and Gordon's works by Zenger.[41]

The author found it a great injustice to "prostitute" two such great men in the name of the freedom of the press.[42] The debate was over how Trenchard and Gordon's works were used. Their essays were printed in the *NYWJ* to gather support against the government. Letters and articles in the *NYG* objected to using Trenchard and Gordon's works to encourage the involvement of the populace in such matters.

By this time, Governor Cosby requested that the General Assembly take action against Zenger because his newspaper had, in Cosby's view, undermined imperial power. The Assembly refused and Cosby went to the Council of the colony of New York, which agreed to have Zenger arrested for seditious libel.[43]

Even though Zenger was in prison, the *NYWJ* kept being printed and on 9 December 1734, the essay titled the "Discourses upon Libels" was repeated.

Both claimed the essential role the freedom of thought, speech, and press played in a free government; and both essays asserted that anyone or anything should not limit this freedom, except that no one should be allowed to violate anyone else's freedom of thought, speech, or press.

Immediately upon Zenger's arrest, James Alexander and William Smith Sr., the two lawyers who represented Rip Van Dam against Cosby in the salary dispute, offered Zenger legal representation. Alexander and Smith first endeavored to convince James DeLancey, the new chief justice appointed by Cosby, to issue reasonable bail for Zenger. After DeLancey flatly refused, Alexander and Smith accused the judge of bias and argued that he should not sit in judgment on the case because of his apparent association with Cosby. DeLancey then disbarred Alexander and Smith for contempt of court. Consequently, Alexander helped Zenger obtain legal council from Andrew Hamilton of Philadelphia, reportedly one of the best trial lawyers in the colonies.[44]

Before the case could be heard, New Yorkers became more involved in the controversy as a result of the press coverage of the case. Two well-selected Trenchard and Gordon essays, numbers 42 and 37, were published in Zenger's newspaper in an attempt to encourage the people of New York to "judge" Governor Cosby's actions.[45] In essay 42, Cato argued that the violation of a "bad" law should be allowed since laws did not make something right or wrong.[46]

The essay stated that there were two laws of human society from which all else derives and they were "equity and self-preservation." By equity, Cato meant that people were "bound alike not to hurt one another." The second law of nature, Cato asserted, was that "all men have a right alike to defend themselves." Furthermore, the essay claimed that the law of nature did not only allow us, "but oblige[d] us, to defend ourselves."[47] Therefore, this essay asserted that a citizen had a duty to defend himself for the sake of society.

In continuation with this last essay's theme, the *NYWJ* reprinted *Cato's Letters* 37 titled "Character of a good and of an evil magistrate, quoted from Algernon Sidney, Esq."[48] The essay propounded that a "good" leader must look out for the welfare of "the people" and not for self-interest. A good magistrate must believe that he was made for the people and not believe that the people were made for him. A good leader was also one who carried out justice and was virtuous. Bad magistrates, according to Cato, were men who were out only for personal gain and used their power against the people. The essay also implored people of a nation to judge the leader for his actions and sustained that it was a duty of people to support good magistrates and reject bad ones. Trenchard and Gordon's essays were used to encourage popular participation in politics.

Finally on 4 August 1735, the Zenger case was heard before a New York jury.[49] At first Zenger's lawyer, Andrew Hamilton, tried to persuade the chief justice that because Zenger was formally charged with "*false*, scandalous, malicious and seditious libel," the prosecution must prove all of those charges. If the judge allowed this argument, then Hamilton had only to prove that the libel was false or was meant to be scandalous, malicious, and seditious. The judge refused Hamilton's request and denied him that line of defense.[50]

Hamilton, therefore, had to take another route to defend Zenger, and relied on an argument from the *Cato's Letters* series to do so. Hamilton's defense came directly from Trenchard and Gordon's essay 38 titled "The Right and Capacity of the People to Judge of Government," which argued that in a "just" government the people must have the right to judge officials as a check against corrupt leaders. Hamilton called Zenger's actions a public duty that all men must engage in so corrupt governors can be exposed.[51]

By arguing against English law, Hamilton relied on the local traditions of New Yorkers. This required the jury to override their allegiance to the crown, and force them to support local customs that allowed citizens to protest against corrupt government officials. The New York jury agreed with Hamilton and found Zenger not guilty. This decision served as an important political precedent; the jury agreed that an informed public was needed to keep government officials in check.[52] Ironically, Hamilton used the words of British writers to uphold colonial customs in direct opposition to British law.

The controversy was far from over at this point; however, the decision in favor of Zenger was a victory for the Morris faction. After the trial, Morris, with the financial support of Rip Van Dam, James Alexander, and William Smith, traveled to London to attempt to depose Cosby.[53]

The "paper war" continued to unfold with Zenger reprinting Trenchard and Gordon's essays. On 25 August 1735, Zenger reprinted essay Number 60 titled "All Government proved to be instituted by men and only to intend the general good of men."[54] Government did not have any power, the essay stated, except what man gave it and no just and free government could be framed without the consent of the people. The essay emphasized that the relationship between government officials and the people should be one of "mutual assistance."

On 1 September 1735, the *NYWJ* continued with the same essay, which further discussed the differences between arbitrary and free governments. In a free government magistrates have their power qualified and "so divided into different channels, and committed to the direction of so many different men, with different interests and views, that the majority of them could seldom or never"[55] agree to perform injustices against the greater good of the people. In contrast, arbitrary governments were "where the rules of publick [sic] power were dictated by private and lawless lust. . . ."[56] The "secret" to a free government, the essay proclaimed, was to make the interests of the governors the same as the interests of the governed. Therefore, if people only support virtuous leaders who act in the public's best interest, leaders will be forced to be virtuous public servants, not the other way around.

The next three issues reprinted Cato 62. The newspaper printed the complete essay titled "An enquiry into the Nature and Extent of Liberty with its loveliness and Advantage, and the vile effects of slavery."[57] This essay specifically defined what liberty meant to the authors and they used a Lockean definition. Liberty was defined as "the power which every man has over his own actions, and his right to enjoy the fruits of his labor, art and industry," the essay stated, "as far as by it he hurts not the society, or any members of it, by taking from any member . . . what he himself enjoys."[58] The essay continued to argue that the sole function of government was to preserve property. Therefore, government should only be concerned with the preservation of private property and government should not be involved in man's private thoughts and actions.

Soon after Cato 62 was printed in the *NYWJ* Morris returned, unsuccessful, from London. As a result of the controversy, however, some reforms took place in the New York colonial government. London instructed Cosby to separate the powers of the legislature and the executive branches of government. Governors of the colony could no longer convene with the Council and have influence over its decisions as Cosby had done when he arranged to have the suit against Zenger heard in court. More frequent elections for the assembly were now required as well, allowing the people more control over the actions of elected assemblymen.[59]

The Zenger controversy ended in 1739 and the *New York Weekly Journal's* last republication of an essay by Trenchard and Gordon, "A vindication of Brutus, for having killed Caesar" occurred on 26 March 1739.[60] This well-chosen essay reached into antiquity to prove its point. The authors asserted that Brutus not only had a right but a duty to kill Caesar because Caesar ruled arbitrarily and had usurped unlimited power. The essay also argued that Caesar was an enemy to all Roman citizens and virtuous men because of his tyrannical rule.

Brutus, the essay declared, had the natural "law of self-preservation, the spirit of the Roman Constitutions, and of those laws of liberty . . ." on his side.[61] The essay was not a cry for the murder of Governor Cosby, because he had already died from natural causes by this time. The essay, however, could be viewed as a final declaration that admonished citizens to judge their rulers and stop at nothing to secure a just government free from arbitrary rule.

The way in which *Cato's Letters* were used during the controversy led readers to view the authors of the essays as freedom of speech advocates who believed people had not only a right but a duty to judge government officials. Overall, this limited message took Trenchard and Gordon's works out of context and emphasized certain selections while eliminating important parts of their works that stressed fear about the people having too much power. The New York optimistic view of "the people" and their ability to preserve liberty was not common in the majority of Trenchard and Gordon's essays, which shows the limited understanding the colonists had of the complete political philosophy of Cato.

Controversy was stirred up again in the colony in the 1750s by the appearance of Trenchard and Gordon's works in a newly created journal called the *Independent Reflector*. Founded by several young prominent New York lawyers, William Livingston, William Smith, Jr. (son of the William Smith, Sr. involved in the Morris-Cosby dispute), and John Morin Scott to improve "the Minds of our Fellow Citizens," the *Reflector* was a series of essays that advocated reforms for a better society. Topics included civil governments, religion, and education.

The *Reflector* also became a forum to air the group's political orientation in local disputes. The most controversial issues of the *Reflector* concerned the heated dispute over the establishment of a publicly funded college in New York that was to be solely controlled by the Anglican Church. Because the *Independent Whig* and select essays from *Cato's Letters* argued against the "corrupt nature" of the church, a few of Trenchard and Gordon's arguments fit well into the debate. During this controversy *Cato's Letters* were summarized or paraphrased on six different occasions, and essays from Trenchard and Gordon's *Independent Whig* appeared seven times.

The first issue of the *Independent Reflector* resembled the introductions to Trenchard and Gordon's *Independent Whig* and *Cato's Letters*. The authors attempted to justify why they were writing the essays and how they intended to complete their task. The main objective, stated the *Reflector*, was "to promote the public welfare."[62] The *Reflector*, like *Cato's Letters* and the *Independent Whig*, discussed civil and religious rights. The authors of the *Independent Reflector* publicized corrupt officeholders, and discussed vice, virtue, slavery, and liberty.[63]

In addition, the authors discussed science and local reforms that might improve the status of the society. The introduction of the *Reflector*, like the introduction of the *Independent Whig*, declared that the authors were not of any one party or faction. Trenchard and Gordon stated: "For my self, who have no manner of attachment to any party, I shall not be afraid to speak my mind of all. . . ."[64] Similarly the authors of the *Reflector* stated "the author being under no attachment to any party, thinks himself the better qualified to make impartial remarks on the conduct of every party."[65]

The *Reflector*'s borrowing from Trenchard and Gordon was eventually chastised in the *New York Mercury*. A letter, signed Dryden, accused the *Reflector* of theft because of the similarity of the *Reflector*'s first essay to the *Independent Whig* Number 1.[66] The scathing essay compared the two texts and as evidence quoted from each of the texts to prove Dryden's point. The objection was to the way the *Reflector* copied from the *Independent Whig*, but did not acknowledge the contribution of Trenchard and Gordon.

The *New York Mercury* was not created as an opposition newspaper. The editor, Hugh Gaine, moved from Ireland to New York and began the *New York Mercury* in 1752 for economic reasons.[67] Gaine, however, found himself in the middle of controversy over King's College. At first Gaine refused to publish anything that involved the conflict but because of public pressure, he was forced to comply. His newspaper served as a voice against the *Reflector*'s position but ended up publishing both sides of the debate.

The *Reflector* began in the pursuit of its original objective. The first and second essays addressed local issues. The first discussed the disapproval of the excise tax and the second addressed "Abuses of the Road."[68] Supposedly, due to these two essays, some people began objecting to the newspaper's political essays.[69] The next essay had a noticeable resemblance to *Cato's Letter* Numbers 38 and 108. The *Reflector* titled the essay "The Different Effects of an absolute and a limited Monarchy: The Glory of a prince ruling according to Law, superior to that of an arbitrary sovereign; with the peculiar Happiness of the British Nation."[70] The essay stated that in limited monarchies the people prospered and enjoyed life. Under a ruler limited in his power, the essay argued, "every thing looks cheerful and happy .... Agriculture is encouraged, and proves the annual source of immense riches to the kingdom." In contrast, under absolute monarchies the "fields lie waste and uncultivated ..." and the leader "wages war against his own subjects."[71]

Reflector Number IX also resembled an essay of *Cato's Letters*. They both said that it was human nature for men to act in self-interest. Government officials, therefore, must be encouraged to act virtuously and the people must support only rulers that promoted the public good. Overall, Cato and the *Reflector* advocated the same argument that rulers must see that it was in their best interest to act for the public good.[72]

The *Reflector* Number XIII similarly resembled *Cato's Letters*. The essay argued against party divisions and stated that factions (party division) appeared when passion took over and the "zeal for the common good, gradually extinguished love of their country." Both the *Reflector* and Trenchard and Gordon referred to party divisions as "political enthusiasm."[73]

The most controversial essays of the *Reflector* appeared between March 1753 and November 1753 and revolved around plans to found a new college in New York, King's College. The debate over the charter for King's College brought both religious and political issues to the surface. The political environment that the conflict created led the writers of the *Independent Reflector* to reprint several selections from Trenchard and Gordon's work, the *Independent Whig*.

The authors of the *Reflector* objected to the establishment of a college that would be funded by the public but controlled by the Episcopal Church. On 22 March 1753 the *Reflector* paraphrased the *Independent Whig* number 5.[74] The essay propounded that it was dangerous for a school to be controlled by a particular church. They believed that religious leaders would "implant the seed of superstition in a tender mind."[75] They argued that freedom of thought could not exist in an institution controlled by the church. The main purpose of a college, announced the *Reflector* and the *Whig*, was to encourage "candid inquiry."

Reflector Number XXXIV, titled "Of the Veneration and Contempt of the Clergy," paraphrased *Independent Whig* Number III. Both essays explained that to revere church leaders as if they were gods was dangerous to a free society. The essays advocated that clergy were men and that all men had the capability of being corrupt. Moreover, clergymen were considered more dangerous than anyone because people revere them simply because of their position in the church and not for their actions.[76]

The next essay in the *Reflector* continued with this subject and closely paraphrased the beginning of *Cato's Letters* essay 45.[77] The essay declared that men were born equal and no man had dominion over another unless the latter surrendered his natural born rights. Similar to Cato's position, liberty was conceptualized as "an inestimable jewel."[78] In conclusion, the essay argued that religious leaders and lay men were both born with the same liberty; therefore, they both must abide by the same laws.[79]

As a result of the controversy over King's College, the authors of the *Reflector* attempted to insert several essays into Hugh Gaine's *New York Mercury*. Gaine, however, refused to involve himself in the dispute. The authors of *Reflector* then submitted their essays to the other New York newspaper, James Parker's *New York Gazette*[80] and they were reprinted. The next *Reflector* addressed Gaine's comment, saying that his "refusal [to print the essays] is an immediate abridgement [sic] of the Freedom of Press." The *Reflector* then proceeded to print an essay titled "Liberty of the Press."[81] In addition, the authors of the *Independent Reflector* republished a 1720 anti-Anglican essay by Thomas Gordon and titled the tract "The Craftsmen: A Sermon from the Independent Whig. . . ."[82]

Gaines quickly responded that he did not violate the freedom of press and he had every right to deny any material he wished from his newspaper. He claimed that the essays had "no other tendency than to display the Author's

Plagiarism, as the two first paragraphs are taken from Vol. 4, No. 287 of Mr. Addison's *Spectator*."[83] Gaine continued: "[they] ought to have given credit for such a procedure, before he caused it to be inserted in the *New-York Gazette* of April 16, 1753."[84] Gaine ended his denunciation with great humor when he made a list of what the *Reflector* "owed" the *Mercury* because the *Reflector* "stole" the works of other people. The list "charged" the *Reflector* with stealing from the *Independent Whig,* Addison's works, and making false accusations against the *Mercury* regarding the freedom of the press.[85] Gaine agreed with Trenchard and Gordon's ideas although he disagreed about how they should be used. Therefore, the argument was not over the literal meaning of their works; but the application of the language allegedly exploited by the publishers and editors.

The next essay in the *Reflector* was titled "A Defence of Ridicule," which stated that "the *Independent Whig* ha[d] gone farther towards shaming tyranny and priestcraft . . . with downright Banter, than could have been effected by austere dogmas, or formal deductions."[86] The *Reflector* asserted that a leader of the church could not teach "truth" because he could not be impartial. The clergy, therefore, should not be allowed to control the college since it would naturally inculcate the students with falsities.[87]

"The Vanity of Birth and Titles; with the Absurdity of claiming Respect without Merit," published in the *Reflector*, also quoted directly from *Cato's Letters* 131.[88] The essay propounded that people must deserve respect before they obtained it and argued that a man in power should not be honored solely because of his position. People were to be judged on their actions and held accountable for them. This section taken from *Cato's Letters* fit perfectly into the controversy over the college because the Anglican Church planned to control the college. The essay addressed the Episcopal Church and said: "I honor Episcopacy; but if a Bishop is a hypocrite, a Time-server, a Traitor a stock-jobber, or a Hunter after power, I shall take leave to scorn the prelate."[89]

On 30 July 1753 an essay in the *New York Mercury* directly addressed the *Reflector*'s arguments against the Anglican Church's power over the college. The anonymous letter claimed that because the colony of New York was a British colony and the Anglican Church was the "established" church, the Church not only had a right to control the college but an obligation to do so.[90]

In response, the *Independent Reflector* borrowed from the *Whig* Number XLIX in an essay titled: "The Argument in support of an ecclesiastical Establishment in this Province, impartially considered, and refuted."[91] The essay stated that the Church of England was not the official established in the colony and even if it was, the government did not "owe its Establishment to any provincial law of our own making."[92] Moreover, the Anglican Church was not the "established" church of Britain since the union of England and Scotland.[93]

This argument brought great opposition, which was voiced in the *New York Mercury*.[94] An anonymous author submitted to the paper an opposition to the *Reflector*'s argument. He wrote, "together with the *Independent Whig*, the *Reflector* has borrowed his false and absurd notions about religion and government."[95] The author continued to assert the necessary role religion played in society and attempted to counter the *Reflector*'s request to separate the church from the college.

The *Reflector* also borrowed from the *Independent Whig* in the essay titled: "Of Credulity."[96] The essay discussed how reason was given to all human beings and should be used to its fullest extent. The authors advocated the need to employ reason to all things in life in order to determine the difference between truth and falsity. The essay rejected the assertion that truth could be found through the teachings of the church alone. In fact, the essay argued that one should question church teachings because God gave every man the capacity to reason independently.[97]

The last two issues of *Independent Reflector* addressed the dispute over the college directly. The terminal issue, published on 22 November 1753, ended the paper war over the establishment of King's College. The influence of Livingston and his group came to an end when Lieutenant Governor DeLancey granted the Anglicans their charter for King's College. DeLancey thought he would gain Anglican support but the opposite occurred. The Anglicans were angry because DeLancey did not stop the *Reflector*'s assault on the college. In addition, Anglicans were incensed over Livingston's political power in the Assembly, which he exercised to deny public funds for the college.[98]

Before the "official" end of the King's College dispute in December of 1756, the *New York Mercury* mentioned Trenchard and Gordon twice. On 3 March 1755 the *Mercury* included several paragraphs quoted directly from Gordon's *Discourses on Tacitus*.[99] The selection made reference to the reasons of why Rome fell, which was because of the corrupt leader Caesar. Then on 15 September 1755 another essay included a glowing compliment to Trenchard and Gordon's works. The essay contended that for "their incomparable writings in favor of virtue and liberty, no men on earth were more calumniated than Gordon and Trenchard."[100] Finally, the King's College dispute ended in 1756 after the Assembly decided to give only half the lottery funds to the college and the other half to the Corporation of the City of New York. In the end, the *Reflector* and its supporters did have an effect on the outcome of the controversy over the establishment of King's College.[101]

The last reprinting of one of Trenchard and Gordon's works in the *New York Mercury* occurred on 21 March 1757. The *Mercury* printed number 27 of *Cato's Letters*, which included a discussion about the effects corruption had on liberty. Trenchard and Gordon were not recognized as the authors;

however, the essay was borrowed from *Cato's Letters*. The essay warned that corruption resulted in tyranny. The essay stated that Roman virtue and liberty expired together. The essay was a plea to the people to be virtuous and only support virtuous leaders or else what happened to Rome would happen to England.[102]

The *Reflector* also influenced the colony of New York because it brought issues of government and religion into the forefront of politics. During the 1750s, the literate public frequently read excerpts from Trenchard and Gordon's works. With the aid of Trenchard and Gordon's works, the *Reflector* not only delayed the establishment of the college but it forced some people to question the role the church should have at the college.[103]

A careful reading reveals that New York printers selected only a few of Trenchard and Gordon's essays to use at particular times when convenient but rejected most of the essays. Trenchard and Gordon's works were found in the middle of two highly politicized controversies in New York before 1760. First, Trenchard and Gordon's *Cato's Letters* appeared in the 1730s during the controversy between Governor Cosby and a group of opponents. Second, their works appeared in the 1750s during the dispute over King's College.

The *New York Weekly Journal* was established to oppose Governor Cosby. This began a paper war between the *NYWJ* and the establishment newspaper, the *New York Gazette*.[104] Trenchard and Gordon's essays fit well into the dispute; therefore, they were reprinted. In response, the *New York Gazette* attacked Zenger's *NYWJ* for perverting Trenchard and Gordon's works. Then the *NYWJ* replied and more accusations were charged. This debate back and forth placed much of Trenchard and Gordon's works in the middle of the controversy. A New Yorker reading about the conflict over the Governor and then over Zenger would know full well who Trenchard and Gordon were and what some of their works represented. Moreover, more people were reading the newspapers because the controversy was so publicized. Therefore, more people probably read Trenchard and Gordon during the 1730s than before or after until the next political dispute in 1750.

In the 1750s, several prominent people placed Trenchard and Gordon's works in the middle of a colonial dispute. The debate over King's College and the arguments of *Cato's Letter* and the *Independent Whig* fit very well into the controversy. Many of the works were pirated and not acknowledged as Trenchard and Gordon's works. Nevertheless, an astute member of the New York colony brought to the attention of the *Mercury* that the *Reflector* had plagiarized from the *Independent Whig*. During the 1750s, too, the literate public was reading a lot from Trenchard and Gordon. Most people in the colony reading about the controversy over King's College knew who Trenchard and Gordon were.

There were several reasons why Trenchard and Gordon's ideology as a *whole* did not influence New Yorkers. First, New York printers only published a select few of Trenchard and Gordon's essays from 1720 to the 1770s. Fewer than 30 of the authors' 144 essays signed "Cato" were reprinted between 1720 and the outbreak of the American Revolution. Second, the few essays that were reprinted portrayed Trenchard and Gordon as optimistic and democratic, which was not an overall message they gave when reading the entire set of their works. Third, people from both sides of various debates cited or borrowed from Trenchard and Gordon's works prior to the American Revolution when convenient. Nonetheless, these essays were important during the 1760s and 1770s for giving colonists a language to oppose British policies and a confidence that "the people" had the ability to preserve liberty. The use of Trenchard and Gordon contributed to a discourse of opposition with limited focus on a specific political philosophy. Their works were taken out of context by their publishers to create an illusion that Trenchard and Gordon supported a democratic society in which the people not only had the right but the duty to judge government officials. As a result, the essays encouraged formally marginalized groups to participate in politics and unintentionally created a political culture based on popular participation.

Contrary to the depiction given by New York printers, the complete political philosophies of Trenchard and Gordon, as written in their *Cato's Letters* series, portrayed two supporters of limited monarchies, very suspicious of businessmen, who held a negative and pessimistic view of humankind. In more than 20 essays, Trenchard and Gordon explained how the majority of people were driven by self-interest, superstition, and passion.[105] In addition, more than 20 essays addressed financial matters such as the South-Sea Bubble crisis, monopolies, stock traders, and the national debt. Not one of these essays was reprinted in New York in the eighteenth century.[106] Instead, New York printers used Trenchard and Gordon's works when applicable to become involved in local political controversies. These colonists chose to reprint the more optimistic essays that portrayed "the people" as the best guardians of liberty. Thus readers believed Trenchard and Gordon's works encouraged the freedoms of speech, press, and the right to judge government officials, especially against corruption.

In the complete set of *Cato's Letters* however, fewer than 10 essays addressed the freedom of speech and press, the right to judge government officials, and positive nature of mankind in the complete set of *Cato's Letters*.[107] Moreover, while Trenchard and Gordon were strong supporters of limited monarchies, their ideas were taken out of context by New Yorkers and used to support republican forms of government.

Trenchard and Gordon's essays were influential but not universal. The Cato that was read in New York was a product not just of what Trenchard and Gordon wrote but of what New Yorkers read and how they read Cato. Trenchard and Gordon's works helped shape opposition thought in New York and this opposition thought also shaped the way Cato was read. Trenchard and Gordon's works were used as a result of people becoming involved in politics, and this in turn encouraged the further development of the popular politics in the colony of New York. Political elites were inadvertently teaching New Yorkers to become active citizens.

NOTES

1. Alan Tully, *Forming American Politics: Ideals, Interests, and Institutions in Colonial New York and Pennsylvania* (Baltimore: The Johns Hopkins University Press, 1994), 213–258.
2. Bernard Bailyn, *The Origins of American Politics* (New York: Vintage Books, 1967), 124. Bailyn asserted that "the history of politics in eighteenth-century America is the history of factionalism." (124). But not all the colonies used newspapers to argue their political debates as in New York and Pennsylvania.
3. Patricia U. Bonomi, *A Factious People: Politics and Society n Colonial New York* (New York: Columbia University Press, 1971), 158.
4. Bonomi, *A Factious People*, 103–139.
5. Gary Nash, "The Transformation of Urban Politics 1700–1765," The *Journal of American History*, Volume 60, Issue 3 (December 1973), 606.
6. Gary Nash, "The Transformation of Urban Politics 1700–1765," 606.
7. William Bradford began his printing career in Philadelphia in the late seventeenth century but moved to New York for political reasons. The "political" reasons involved Bradford being charged with printing seditious libel. Ironically, Bradford ended up serving as the voice of the "establishment" in a case involving John Peter Zenger allegedly committing libel against the Governor of New York.
8. Vincent Buranelli. "Peter Zenger's Editor" *American Quarterly* vol. 7, issue 2 (Summer 1955), 174–181.
9. Vincent Buranelli. "Peter Zenger's Editor." *American Quarterly*, 174–181. Buranelli uncovered a letter written by Governor Cosby to the Duke of Newcastle that showed his distaste for James Alexander only a month after Cosby's arrival in the colony. Cosby said Alexander was unfit to be on the New York and New Jersey Councils and he said that he was "the only man that has given me any uneasiness since my arrival." Letter from Governor Cosby to the Duke of Newcastle, December 18, 1732. *Documents Relative to the Colonial History of the State of New York*, ed. E. B. O'Callaghan (Albany: Weed, Parsons, 1853–87) 940.
10. *Cato's Letters*, Numbers 15, 38, and 131.
11. *Cato's Letters,* Number 15.

12. The essay is attributed to Cato; yet, it was not one of the 144 in the *Cato's Letters* series. According to Buranelli this essay was from *The Craftsman*, p. 121. Bolingbroke. The editor probably made a mistake by not crediting the proper author.

13. A free government was defined as a government that was based on laws; not a government based on arbitrary measures.

14. *New York Weekly Journal* (*NYWJ*), 12 November 1733.

15. *NYWJ*, 19 November 1733.

16. *NYWJ*, 10 December 1733. *Cato's Letters*, Number 38.

17. *NYWJ*, 10 December 1733. *Cato's Letters*, Number 38.

18. *NYWJ*, 10 December 1733. *Cato's Letters*, Number 38.

19. *NYWJ*, 31 December 1733. *Cato's Letters*, Number 131.

20. *New York Gazette*, 28 January -4 February 1733. Number 432.

21. There are only a few small quotations taken from Gordon's *Tacitus*. *Cato's Letters* were reprinted far more than Gordon's *Tacitus* was.

22. After Trenchard's death in 1723, Gordon had been accused of taking bribes from Sir Robert Walpole who had fueled much of the opposition literature Trenchard and Gordon wrote. Soon after 1723 Gordon was made First Commissioner of Wine Licenses by the Walpole administration. Gordon then dedicated the rest of his personal life to translating *Tacitus*. Gordon also wrote a two-hundred-page preface in which he summarized his political views in less enflamed prose. See Hamowy, Introduction.

23. *New York Gazette*, 28 January-4 February 1733 Number 432.

24. *New York Gazette*, 28 January-4 February 1733 Number 432.

25. For the most part this is true. There are a few paragraphs that were left out of the essays but they were usually examples that did not change the meaning of the essay.

26. Clark argued that the reprinting of *Cato's Letters* did not propel the Governor to accuse Zenger of seditious libel. Rather, the "letters to the public" he printed that directly attacked the governor was the reason for the charges against him. *The Public Prints*, 183.

27. *NYWJ*, 18 February 1733. *Cato's Letters*, Number 15.

28. *NYWJ*, 18 February 1733. *Cato's Letters*, Number 15.

29. Elizabeth Christine Cook, *Literary Influences in Colonial Newspapers 1704–1750*. New York: Kennikat Press, 1966. Bradford also used Collier's *Moral Essays*, Hooker's *Ecclesiastical Polity*, and the Earl of Clarendon's *History of the Rebellion* to counter Zenger's newspaper essays, 137.

30. *NYWJ*, 25 February 1733. *Cato's Letters*, Number 32.

31. *NYWJ*, 4 March 1733. *Cato's Letters*, Number 32.

32. *NYWJ*, 11 March 1733. *Cato's Letters*, Number 33 "Cautions against the Natural Encroachment of power."

33. *NYWJ*, 11 March 1733. *Cato's Letters*, Number 33.

34. *NYWJ*, 11 March 1733. *Cato's Letters*, Number 33.

35. *NYWJ* March 11, 1733. *Cato's Letters*, Number 33.

36. *New York Gazette*, 18 March-25 March 1734 Number 439.

37. *New York Gazette*, 18 March-25 March 1734 Number 439.

38. *New York Gazette*, 18 March-25 March 1734 Number 439.

39. This was the first time the *NYWJ* reprinted part of two essays in one issue. *NYWJ* May 27, 1734 Numbers 75 and 115.

40. *NYWJ*, 27 May 1734.
41. *New York Gazette*, 21 October-28 October 1734 Number 470.
42. *New York Gazette*, 21 October-28 October 1734 Number 470.
43. Bailyn, *Origins of American Politics*. Councilmen were appointed, not elected, and therefore would find favor with the man who controlled their position. New York, like some colonial governments in the eighteenth century, tried to set up a similar governmental structure to that of England. The Governor was the counterpart to the King in England, the Council equated with the House of Lords, and the House of Commons correlated to the colonial Assembly. Because of local circumstances, the New York government did not function the same as the English government. The governor often could not "play politics" like the King could with his House of Lords and Commons in England. Therefore, conflict in some of the colonies oftentimes broke out between the Governor, Council, and the Assemblies.
44. Bonomi, *A Factious People*, 116–119. Also see Stanley Katz's *Introduction to James Alexander's Brief Narrative of the Case and Trial of John Peter Zenger* (Cambridge, 1963).
45. *NYWJ*, 7 July 1735. *Cato's Letters*, Number 42.
46. *NYWJ*, 7 July 1735. *Cato's Letters*, Number 42.
47. *NYWJ*, 7 July 1735. *Cato's Letters*, Number 42.
48. *NYWJ*, 21 July 1735, *Cato's Letters*, Number 37. Algernon Sidney was a popular hero in the late seventeenth century and throughout the eighteenth century. He was famous for his controversial doctrines on government. During the Exclusion crisis, Sidney and other leading Whigs tried to exclude the Catholic heir to the throne, James Duke of York. Their efforts failed; therefore, Sidney and others planned to revolt. Before the revolt occurred, Sidney was arrested and charged with treason. He was found guilty and executed on 7 December 1683. See Algernon Sidney's *Discourses Concerning Government* edited by Thomas G. West. (Indianapolis, Indiana: Liberty Fund), 1996.
49. For years historians believed that the Zenger trial was about the freedom of press. It was once thought that attorney Hamilton argued that Zenger had a right to publish material against the Governor because it was true. However, English Common Law regarding seditious libel did not allow unfavorable material to be published about the government even if it was in fact true. Moreover, Cosby's actions were typical in the British Empire and were used by many people in the imperial administration.
50. *A Brief Narrative of the Case and Trial of John Peter Zenger, Printer of the New York Weekly Journal for a Libel*. (New York: by John Holt in 1770.) First printed by Zenger in 1736.
51. *A Brief Narrative of the Case and Trial of John Peter Zenger, Printer of the New York Weekly Journal for a Libel*. (New York: by John Holt in 1770.) First printed by Zenger in 1736.
52. Leonard W. Levy. *Emergence of a Free Press* (NY: Oxford University Press, 1985), 37–45. Also see Stanley Katz's Introduction to James Alexander's *Brief Narrative of the Case and Trial of John Peter Zenger* (Cambridge, 1963). Michael Warner, *The Letters of the Republic: Publication and the Public Sphere in Eighteenth-Century America* (Cambridge, MA: Harvard University Press, 1990), 54.
53. Morris did not succeed.
54. *NYWJ*, 25 August 1735. *Cato's Letters*, Number 60.

55. *NYWJ*, 1 September 1733.

56. *NYWJ*, 1 September 1733.

57. *NYWJ*, 8, 15, 23, September 1735. *Cato's Letters*, Number 62.

58. Private Property was defined as lands, goods, and the "fruits of one's labor."

59. The more frequent elections are, the more public electors are subject to removal. Therefore, if an elected official wants to obtain reelection, he will keep his electorates' concerns more in mind. *Cato's Letters* Number 61: "So that I can see no means in human policy to preserve the publick [sic] liberty and a monarchical form of government together, but by the frequent fresh elections of the people's deputies: This is what the writers in politicks [sic] call rotation of magistracy."

60. *NYWJ*, 26 March 1739. *Cato's Letters*, Number 56.

61. *NYWJ*, 26 March 1739. *Cato's Letters*, Number 56.

62. Milton Klein, ed, *The Independent Reflector, or Weekly Essays on Sundry Important subjects more particularly Adapted to the Province of New York* (New Boston: The Belknap Press of Harvard University Press, 1963), 57.

63. *Cato's Letters* began as "an honest and humane intention, to call for public justice upon the wicked managers of the late South Sea scheme." Preface of *Cato's Letters*, 11.

64. Milton Klein, ed, *The Independent Reflector*, 57.

65. Milton Klein, ed, *The Independent Reflector*, 57.

66. *The New York Mercury*, 28 May 1753. *Cato's Letters*, Number 40.

67. Isaiah Thomas. *History of Printing in America, with a Biography of Printers in two volumes*. New York: Burt Franklin, 1964. First published in Albany 1874. Page 300–301. Volume 1.

68. *Cato's Letters* also included sections on taxes. Number 10 gave a similar argument in that a country must not tax labor or industry to the point of discouraging it. *The Reflector* made a similar argument that it was "more reasonable to tax the Luxury, than the Industry of a people."

69. Klein, ed, *The Independent Reflector*, Introduction.

70. *Independent Reflector*, Number IV 21 December 1752.

71. *Independent Reflector*, Number IV 21 December 1752.

72. *Independent Reflector*, Number IX 25 January 1753 and *Cato's Letters*, Numbers 31 and 115.

73. *Independent Reflector* Number XIII 22 February 1753. And in *Cato's Letters* see Numbers 80 and 96.

74. *Independent Reflector* Number XVII 22 March 1753. *Independent Whig* Number 5.

75. *Independent Reflector* Number XVII 22 March 1753. *Independent Whig* Number 5.

76. *Reflector*, Number XXXIV 19 July 1753. *Independent Whig*, Number III. This essay also shows resemblance to *Cato's Letters*, Number 131.

77. *Reflector*, Number XXXVI 2 August 1753. Essay titled: "The Absurdity of the Civil Magistrate's interfering in Matters of Religion." *Cato's Letters* Number 45 titled "Of the Equality and Inequality of men." The first paragraph began: "Men are naturally equal, none ever rose above the rest but by force or consent: No man was

ever born above the rest, nor below them all; and therefore there never was any man in the world so good or so bad, so high or so low, but he had his fellow. Nature is a kind and benevolent parent; she constitutes rest; but for the most part sends all her offspring into the world furnished with the elements of understanding and strength, to provide for themselves. . . ."

78. *Reflector* XXXVI 2 August 1753 and *Cato's Letters*, Number 45.

79. *Reflector* XXXVI and *Reflector* XXXVIII.

80. James Parker was born in Woodbridge, New Jersey and was an apprentice of William Bradford in New York. In 1742 Parker took over Bradford's shop and newspaper. See Thomas's *History of Printing*, 297–298.

81. *Reflector* Number XL 30 August 1753. "Of the Use, Abuse, and Liberty of the Press." Not copied from Trenchard and Gordon since they never wrote a letter with a primary theme of the liberty of the press. However, the tone of *Cato's Letters* Number 15 "Of Freedom of Speech: That the same is inseparable from public Liberty" was very similar to the *Reflector*'s.

82. See footnotes in Klein, ed, *The Independent Reflector*, 343.

83. *New York Mercury*, 3 September 1753.

84. *New York Mercury*, 3 September 1753.

85. *New York Mercury*, 3 September 1753. Number 56. "For stealing from the *Independent Whig*, Lies 10 . . . for stealing from Mr. Addison and others, 16 . . . Their Rage for the Liberty of the Press, when its liberty was never invaded, they having Freedom to chuse [sic] two others 10." The borrowing from other authors did not seem to be a problem until it was used to undermine someone's position on a political matter. However, the *New York Mercury* editor argued that the editors of the *Reflector* should have acknowledged that they borrowed sections from Trenchard and Gordon's works.

86. The fact that the *Reflector* decided to name the *Independent Whig* was probably due to the criticism the periodical was getting from the *Mercury* and its contributors. *Reflector*, Number XLI 6 September 1753.

87. *Reflector*, Number XLI 6 September 1753.

88. *Reflector* Number XLIII 20 September 1753. And *Cato's Letters* Number 131. The *Reflector* acknowledged that they took the quote from *Cato's Letters*. Klein noted that this essay would seem to be paradoxical for Livingston to print because Livingston is part of a New York aristocratic family. Klein, however, asserted that "from youth to manhood, he [Livingston] expressed constant irritation with 'high life,' with the 'fobberies of dress, and the airy diversions of the gay world,' and with the 'vain formality of fools.'"

89. *Reflector* Number XLIII 20 September 1753. And *Cato's Letters* Number 131.

90. *New York Mercury*, 30 July 1753. Ned C. Landsman, "Nation, Migration, and the Province in the First British Empire: Scotland and the Americas, 1600–1800," *The American Historical Review*, Vol. 104, Issue 2 (April, 1999), 463–475. Landsman argued that as a result of the Act of Union in 1707, the Church of England was no longer the establishment church. See Francis Makemie case on page 472.

91. *Reflector* Number XLIV 27 September 1753. *Whig* Number XLIX. Titled "An Inquiry into Religious Establishments, with a further confutation of the impious and absurd claims of high priests."

92. *Reflector* Number XLIV 27 September 1753.

93. *Reflector* Number XLIV 27 September 1753. See Landsman "Nation, Migration, and the Province in the First British Empire: Scotland and the Americas, 1600–1800." Because Scotland and England joined in the Act of Union of 1707 and Scotland was Presbyterian, not Anglican, the British Empire did not have one established church.

94. *New York Mercury,* 24 September 1753 Number 59.

95. *New York Mercury,* 24 September 1753 Number 59.

96. *Reflector* Number XLVII 18 October 1753. *Whig* Number XXVII and Number XXXV. The essay before this one was said by Klein to have been taken from the *Whig*. However, I find the match a poor one, therefore, I left it out.

97. *Reflector,* Number XLVII 18 October 1753.

98. Klein, ed, *The Independent Reflector,* 43–45.

99. *New York Mercury,* 3 March 1755.

100. *New York Mercury,* 15 September 1755. The quote continued: ". . . nor will their memories for these very writings cease to be honored by posterity, while their remains either good sense or gratitude in the nation."

101. Klein, ed, *The Independent Reflector,* 43–45.

102. *New York Mercury,* 21 March 1757. *Cato's Letters,* Number 27.

103. Klein, 385. Apparently the Anglican members of the founding group of the college had asked Governor George Clinton for a charter of incorporation but he turned them down. This was inconsistent with Clinton's political orientation. Clinton and the Livingstons often found themselves on opposing sides of issues. In addition, when two new bills for raising additional funds for the college were introduced into the Assembly during the summer of 1753, several members expressed their suspicions of the composition of the board, which was administrating the money. Livingston was disappointed that the bills still passed but he was pleased that his writings encouraged some people to question the religious leaders of the college.

104. The establishment newspaper was the paper that printed the official news of the colony.

105. *Cato's Letters*, Numbers 8, 13, 19, 27, 31, 40, 43–45, 49, 51–52, 57, 82, 85, 105, 115, 117, 123, 134.

106. *Cato's Letters*, Numbers 2–10, 20–21, 64, 67, 68, 86–92, 107.

107. *Cato's Letters*, Numbers 15, 22, 24, 32, 38, 60–61, 89.

Chapter Five

Trenchard and Gordon's Works in Pennsylvania Newspapers Before 1760

Trenchard and Gordon's works were reprinted in Pennsylvania newspapers more often than in any other colony's newspapers. Their works, especially *Cato's Letters*, appeared quite consistently from the 1720s to 1760.[1] Over fifty essays from the *Cato's Letters* collection were reprinted in periodicals such as the *American Weekly Mercury, Pennsylvania Gazette*, and the *Pennsylvania Journal*. Because Cato's essays were reprinted so frequently in the colony, Pennsylvania is a good case study of how colonists employed and interpreted Trenchard and Gordon's works in the eighteenth century. This study also indicates why *Cato's Letters* were reprinted and the influence their letters had on Pennsylvania society.

Essays from the *Cato's Letters* series were reprinted in well-established newspapers when controversies arose between the two opposing groups in the Pennsylvania government—the proprietor and the assembly. Beginning in the 1720s, these two groups realized the importance of gaining popular support from the middling and lower classes and immigrant groups.[2] The structure of the Pennsylvania government allowed for this expansion of popular politics. By 1720, the colony's governmental structure consisted of a governor and council all appointed by the proprietor, and an assembly elected by popular vote. Because the assembly was elected, it became important for politicians to recruit the support of people outside the traditional elite voting community. In order to include these groups in the political process, politicians employed the press to entice the populace to the polls. Newspapers and pamphlets were an efficient way to reach a wider audience. These newspapers could be read individually, within the family, amongst friends and in taverns. This gave the middling and lower classes access to political discourse that reached beyond their immediate circles of acquaintance.[3] A significant amount of the political literature that was published in Pennsylvania newspapers was borrowed from

Trenchard and Gordon's political tracts, *Cato's Letters*. Because the proprietary supporters, Quakers, and governor supporters printed political literature that attempted to gain popular support, they oftentimes all used Trenchard and Gordon's works to their advantage.

For example, an economic crisis broke out in Pennsylvania in the 1720s, which resulted in the attempt of Governor William Keith to gain popular support among the lower classes by his enactment of new economic policies. Governor Keith, with the help of printer Andrew Bradford, used the *American Mercury* to encourage more people to become involved in policies enacted by the government. The *Mercury* reprinted essays arguing in favor of Keith's paper currency plan and included several political essays. Bradford printed ten essays from Trenchard and Gordon's *Cato's Letters* series. These essays included subjects such as the right to judge government officials, human nature, and public spirit.

Again in 1728, a battle ensued involving the Governor of Pennsylvania but this time it was between Governor Patrick Gordon and assemblyman Andrew Hamilton.[4] This controversy led to the reprinting of several Cato essays in two opposing newspapers, the *American Mercury* and the *Pennsylvania Gazette*. Both attempted to gain popular support for their cause. Another dispute in the late 1750s resulted in the use of *Cato's Letters* in the Pennsylvania press. The dispute was over the power of habeas corpus in the assembly. People in favor of and against the issue printed political essays, letters, and pamphlets attempting to gain support from the populace.

The political culture in Pennsylvania evolved dramatically during the early to mid-eighteenth century and Trenchard and Gordon's works played a significant role in that change. The development of popular politics encouraged the reprinting of some of their essays. The reprinting of their political works, in return, reinforced the increase of popular politics in Pennsylvania.

The first controversy that led to the reprinting of select essays by Trenchard and Gordon was the result of an economic crisis that began in the 1720s. The controversy began a few years after the proprietor, William Penn, appointed William Keith governor in 1715. Keith capitalized on the confusion over the proprietary title and on an economic recession to promote his own interests.[5] Keith thought that the crown would eventually acquire Pennsylvania, which would have made Pennsylvania a royal colony. Keith, therefore, attempted to acquire popular support in the colonies because he thought that once ownership shifted to the crown then the elected assembly would have more power than the council, which was appointed by the Penn family.[6] Keith sought support from lower-class workingmen in Philadelphia and German and Scotch-Irish immigrants.[7]

In this environment Philadelphia's first newspaper, the *American Weekly Mercury*, was established. Andrew Bradford founded the *American Weekly*

Mercury in 1719.⁸ Bradford supported a plan that Governor William Keith advocated involving the printing of paper currency to alleviate Pennsylvania's economic problems. The people supporting the proprietary interests and conservative wealthy Quakers, mainly members from the appointed Council, vehemently opposed the idea of printing paper money because it would cause inflation and cheapen the debts that most people owed to the proprietors of the colonies in taxes and quitrents.⁹ Pennsylvanians were divided on this issue based on economic status. The middling and poorer economic members of society supported the paper money scheme to help alleviate their debts while the wealthier Pennsylvanians objected because they were the ones who held the loans.¹⁰

In response to the opposition to the paper currency plan, Keith and David Lloyd (Speaker of the Assembly) rallied many of the common people and began to question the authority of the council and said that it had no place in Pennsylvania's constitution. Keith, Lloyd, and their supporters contended that the provincial government was only composed of an executive, the governor, and the elected assembly, the people. They said that the council was a body that existed to advise the governor only when asked.

Bradford used his *American Weekly Mercury* to support Keith's plan to print paper currency. Bradford printed a controversial tract that demanded the government do something to help alleviate the effects of the crisis by the issuance of paper currency.¹¹ Bradford was immediately brought before the council in Pennsylvania on charges of printing seditious libel against the government. On 1 February 1721 Bradford argued before the council that he was unaware of the pamphlet. In response to the charge against the issue of the *Mercury* that supported the scheme he said his "journey-man, who composed the said Paper, without his knowledge" printed it.¹²

The council accepted Bradford's defense probably because of the popularity of the new paper currency plan among the populace and the support that it had from Governor Keith. The Council pardoned him; however, Bradford was forbidden to publish anything that concerned the affairs of the government.¹³

By the record alone, one would be led to believe that Bradford yielded to the Council's wishes.¹⁴ Articles written in his *Mercury,* however, reveal a different picture. The very astute Bradford began printing essays written by Trenchard and Gordon seemingly to address the economic depression and the role that the provincial government should take to alleviate the problems.¹⁵ Bradford believed he was the voice of the people and he used Trenchard and Gordon's essays to justify his role as a printer in Pennsylvania society. By reprinting *Cato's Letters* Number 38 titled "The Right and Capacity of the people to judge of Government,"¹⁶ Bradford argued that it was his duty to inform the public on political matters. Trenchard and Gordon, in Cato Number

38, explained that a leader must be concerned with the public good and there must be a mutual trust between the people and the leader. Trenchard and Gordon encouraged people to interfere with government in order to keep government officials from taking advantage of citizens. Moreover, the essay asserted that it was the "duty of every individual to be concerned for the whole, in which himself is included."[17]

The economic recession led to a questioning of the role the provincial government should play in financial matters. This provoked discussions within the colony and Bradford used this opportunity to discuss subjects such as the nature of humans, the danger of corruption, public spirit, characteristics of "good" rulers, and the role of the Church.[18]

After Bradford's initial essay that justified his importance as a newspaper printer, he discussed the subject of human nature. Essay number 40 was reprinted after the Council's direct castigation of the paper money scheme.[19] This essay implicitly addressed the Council's objections to the paper money scheme. The members of the Council who objected to the plan were large property owners and creditors. Bradford, therefore, used this essay to insinuate that these members would not see that it was in their best interest to help debtors with the issuance of paper currency. The overall intention of the essay was to explain that it was human nature for people to be corrupt and selfish. The essay contended that people were never satisfied and they always strove to acquire more property and power. The essay labeled this idea the "nature of man." People had a tendency to state that once they acquired a certain amount of wealth or power, they would stop. Because of human nature, however, that would not happen.[20]

Bradford also reprinted Cato 33 on the subject of human nature.[21] The essay declared that it was human nature to acquire as much power as possible and therefore there was no such thing as too much restraint on power. Since the Council members were appointed and the voting people in Pennsylvania did not check their power, Bradford believed the members had dangerous unrestrained power.[22] Consequently, men who were not held accountable for their actions would naturally act unaccountably.

Because it was a man's will to exercise "dominion over all," there must be laws and magistrates that had the ability to limit the power of these men. Men could never be trusted to "execute the laws upon himself."[23] Moreover, the essay avowed that men "seldom or never stop at certain degrees of mischief, when they have power to go further; but hurry on from wickedness to wickedness. . . ."[24] In conclusion the essay affirmed that government was supposed to be a "mutual contract" between men and rulers and that government was based on laws and men should give up some of their natural liberty to gain "civil security."[25]

Bradford reprinted *Cato's Letters* 134, which argued that it was human nature for society to divide into factions or parties. By the end of 1723, the economic recession had resulted in a clear formulation of factions dividing between people who supported the Governor and those who did not.

One could infer that since Bradford made his position clear, he would have been criticized for being a "party" advocate.[6] Whether or not that was the case, Bradford believed that he needed to make a statement against parties and factions. Bradford found *Cato's Letters* 134 appropriate to reprint in his *Mercury*. The essay reviewed the dangers of parties or factions. The essay assured that men who joined parties usually were blinded by the support they gave to that party.

A party leader could win someone over by giving him a drink and this was dangerous, the essay cautioned. One should make decisions that are "governed by judgment," not by sensations. Cato stated that parties and factions encouraged people to make decisions based on emotions, which was dangerous to a free country. In conclusion, people could be easily tricked and taken advantage of, therefore, people should avoid supporting parties and factions.[27]

Public spirit was another subject that Bradford used selections from *Cato's Letters* to discuss.[28] The essay defined public spirit as the "love of one's country." The essay drew a difference between what the authors called arbitrary countries and free countries. Public spirit in arbitrary countries was "to be blind slaves to the blind will of the Prince."[29] On the contrary, the authors reasoned that public spirit was different in Protestant countries. Public spirit in free countries was to "reconcile the true interest of the governed and governors; it [was] to expose *impostors*,[30] and to resist oppressors." Bradford also reprinted two essays that further lauded Protestant nations as opposed to Catholic countries. *Cato's Letters* 128 argued that the Catholic Church was a corrupt institution and that the "priestcraft and tyranny are ever inseparable and go hand-in-hand."[31]

The discussion continued with the declaration that public spirit in free countries must be maintained by both leaders and citizens in order to preserve "liberty, plenty, ease, and security."[32] Along a similar theme, Bradford reprinted Essay Number 34 that discussed the fallacy of some people who flatter rulers in the name of public spirit.[33] Flattery was defined as a "pernicious weed, which grows and prevails everywhere. . . ."[34] People who truly love their country will not support rulers who do not make decisions in the favor of the public good. Loyalty to one's country, therefore, should be directly related to supporting rulers who act in the interests of all, rather than for selfish reasons. There was a difference, Cato said, between loyalty to a "good" prince and loyalty to a "bad" prince. The essay argued that to obey a leader who followed the law could be called loyalty. On the contrary, if one obeyed a leader who did not follow the law—that was not considered loyalty.[35]

Bradford then discussed the notion that one should respect only rulers who act in the best interest of the whole. Essay 131 stated that respect should be given only to men with true qualities who carried out good actions. The authors frowned upon honoring men just because they wore certain clothes or held a powerful position. Trenchard and Gordon showed their humor with an example from ancient Greece. The authors announced that the Greeks took great pride in their beards but they said goats oftentimes had beards just as great. Hence, the beard does not make the man. The essay further explained that it was ridiculous to revere someone because they carried a "long staff" and they should be laughed at. One must honor a person only for the actions that are "good." Furthermore, one must deserve reverence before one could claim it.[36]

The politicians' attempt to gain support from a wider audience led to the increased use of the press and influenced the political discourse in Pennsylvania. Essays that encouraged the people to judge government officials, discussions about human nature and corruption, along with essays on public spirit were widely circulated in Pennsylvania newspapers in an attempt to gain the attention of interested readers. Trenchard and Gordon's essays helped foster the development of a new political culture. Because Trenchard and Gordon's essays were simple and highly polemic, people from the middling and lower status could understand their arguments quite well and probably found them interesting to read.

In March of 1729, another controversy ensued that encouraged people to become involved in politics. The battle for power occurred between Andrew Hamilton, a powerful assemblyman, and the governor, Patrick Gordon.[7] This dispute caused a stir in the colony.[38] The *American Mercury* reprinted several of Trenchard and Gordon's works to voice its opposition to Hamilton in favor of Governor Gordon. Governor Gordon desired to rid Hamilton of his position in the Assembly. Gordon was able to dissuade voters from supporting Hamilton in an election to keep him in the Assembly.[39] Andrew Bradford opposed Hamilton in favor of Governor Gordon. Bradford made his position clear by printing several of Trenchard and Gordon's Cato essays. In Hamilton's defense, Benjamin Franklin's *Pennsylvania Gazette*[40] also reprinted some of Trenchard and Gordon's works.[41] Moreover, Andrew Hamilton was also a firm supporter of Trenchard and Gordon's works as seen in 1735 when he defended John Peter Zenger in New York and used their works to win the case.[42] Both sides of this dispute used the ideas of Trenchard and Gordon, which signifies the dual usage of their works by two opposing groups vying for popular support.

In 1729, the Assembly ordered Bradford to be arrested for printing against the government. After being released, in protest Bradford reprinted

Cato's Letters 100 titled "Discourses upon Libels" on 13 March 1729. The essay confirmed that libels played an important role in society because they revealed the behavior of government officials. Because it was a duty for people to judge government officials, the freedom of speech and writing were necessary liberties. Therefore, without the liberty to speak against the government, people would not have the proper tools to perform their responsibility to keep leaders in check. The essay also explained that it was better for a society to suffer from false libels than to deny the freedom of speech and press.[43] Bradford viewed his role in society as educator of the public to expose corrupt government officials.

Bradford also printed other essays from *Cato's Letters* that could be seen as a justification for his role as printer in a free society. On 5 March 1734 Bradford reprinted Cato 15.[44] He began the essay with rhetoric on the freedom of press and then continued by reprinting Cato's essay on the subject of speech freedom. The first paragraph stated that the freedom of press was a "sacred privilege" that "our English Cato [believed was] so essential to free governments that the security of property, and the freedom of speech always go together."[45] The fiery tone increased when the essay contended that "those wretched countries where a man cannot call his tongue his own, he can scarce call any thing else his own."[46] Furthermore, the essay cautioned that when someone desired to take over a country he always began with subduing the freedom of speech. Throughout the past, Cato argued, tyrants always found the freedom of speech a nuisance and a threat to their power. They always advocated punishing writers and speakers by violent means for revealing the truth. Trenchard and Gordon warned that when truth became a crime in a country, liberty no longer existed. The freedom of speech, therefore, was "the great bulwark of liberty; they prosper and die together," proclaimed Cato.[47]

Furthering this line of argument, Bradford reprinted *Cato's Letters* 102, which linked the freedom of speech and press with the duty that people have to check government officials. The essay held that it was human nature for people to seek wealth and as long as the pursuit was "just and proper," people were virtuous. If someone acquired wealth by dishonest means, however, he should not be complimented. A person's desires, therefore, did not determine whether or not a person acted virtuously, it was the end result of the person's desires that decided the nature of his actions. As long as society only respected people who carried out their desires in moderation and in truth, than society would remain free. In contrast, if society supported people who advocated corrupt behavior, the society was not safe from arbitrary rulers. If the desire for wealth and the importance of reputation were in balance, people would be "happy." Wicked men, however, were never meant to be happy no matter how much wealth or power they obtained.[48]

Several times during this almost ten-year dispute, Bradford used select essays of Trenchard and Gordon to address an upcoming election in the Assembly, of which Hamilton was a member and to which he frequently stood for reelection. A few days before an Assembly election in 1729 Bradford printed an essay that borrowed ideas from *Cato's Letters* 39. The essay was part of the Busy-Body series authored by Joseph Breintnall.[49] The essay quoted directly from Trenchard and Gordon on the subject of passion. "There [was] scarce any one of the passions but what [was] truly laudable, when it center[ed] in the public, and [made] that it's [sic] object," the essay contended.[50] The essay also discussed the corrupt nature of power and the "dangers" that arose from private passions. In addition, the essay averred the need for rotation in office to protect the society against the corrupt nature of leaders.[51]

Since the essay was published so close to the Assembly election, Hamilton and his supporters in the Council suspected the essay was directed at them. The Council, upon the request of Hamilton, arrested Bradford for some unknown time.[52] As soon as Bradford was released, on 25 September 1729, he again printed a Busy-Body essay that borrowed from *Cato's Letters* 69 and 70. The essay declared that it was not only a right but a duty for "freeholders" to judge government officials. The essay also dared to mention the approaching election and advised the voters to be sure to judge the former representatives' actions and make sure to support only those who represented the public good.[53] Interestingly, Andrew Hamilton used this very same argument in his defense of Zenger. Moreover, this argument was what ended up winning the case against Zenger's seditious libel charge.[54]

Bradford again used Trenchard and Gordon's works to comment on an Assembly election. Four days before the annual election on 27 September 1733, the *Mercury* printed an essay signed "Cato Jun," which imitated *Cato's Letters* 38. The letter read:

> To the Freemen. My Dear Countrymen,
> As the time draws nigh of choosing our Representatives in the Legislative capacity; let us duely [sic] consider, that the Trust to be reposed in them, it is of the greatest Importance and requires Persons of Known Integrity, Ability, Discretion and Resolution to discharge it faithfully; for they are the Guardians of our valuable liberties, which, as we are freeborn, it is our interest and Duty to preserve, not only for our selves but also for the Benefit of posterity.[55]

The essay continued to discuss the elements necessary for a government to be considered free. The essay advocated the need for a constitution so that power would be restrained and liberty could prevail. Arbitrary governments existed where there were no constitutions. The essay also claimed that government representatives must be forced to be virtuous by the freemen of society.[56]

Three days later, after the Assembly election, Bradford again printed an essay in the *Mercury* signed Cato Jr. The essay began with the phrase: "when the wicked perish there [was] shouting."[57] The article continued by thanking the people of Pennsylvania for making a "brave stand . . . against lawless and arbitrary power."[58] Immediately following the essay was a list of who won the election for the Assembly and Andrew Hamilton, one of the leading proprietary party supporters, was not among the members.[59]

Several essays that Bradford reprinted addressed the increase of deferential society that arose in Pennsylvania between 1726 and 1755. By the mid-1720s Pennsylvania had an established provincial elite.[60] A sub-set of this group gained sufficient political and economic power and they demanded deference. This group was composed mainly of wealthy Quakers but also some wealthy Anglicans. Bradford, therefore, was attacking both the Quaker and Anglican leaders such as Andrew Hamilton when he reprinted *Cato's Letters* 45. The essay rejected a hierarchical system of society and government. The essay confirmed that men were naturally born equal and no one could be above another by nature. The essay proclaimed that it was not in every person's future to be great, however, everyone had the capability of being virtuous. "To be great, [was] not in every man's power; but to be good, [was] in the power of all," Trenchard and Gordon expounded.[61]

Along with the protest against this social elite group, Bradford used *Cato's Letters* 123 titled "Inquiry Concerning Madness, especially religious Madness called Enthusiasm" to address the Quakers further. The essay protested against religious zealots because they were accused of not using reason to make decisions. Under the auspices of religion, people took advantage of other people, stated Cato. Trenchard and Gordon wrote that enthusiasts were impostors and should be considered "madmen" by all. They emphasized the need to use reason to curb the urge to support enthusiasts.[62]

On 21 May 1730, Bradford boldly reprinted Cato essay 124 titled "Further Reasoning upon Enthusiasm." This essay directly addressed Quakerism. By reprinting this essay, Bradford openly displayed his anti-Quaker views. The essay propounded that Quakers were enthusiasts and that they were dangerous to society because they persuaded themselves and others that they represented God. Bradford, being a devout Anglican, found Quaker practices "dangerous." The Trenchard and Gordon essay again emphasized the need for reason when dealing with religions. They believed that God had given people reason for the sole purpose for people to use. The essay stated: "Almighty God . . . has given us reason to distinguish truth from falsehood, imposture from revelation, delusion from inspiration; and when we quit that light we must wander through endless mazes and dark labyrinths. . . ."[63]

On 27 April 1738 the *Mercury* printed another essay that summarized two of *Cato's Letters*.[64] The essay began with the argument that people had not only the right but also the *duty* to judge government officials, therefore, encouraging popular politics. The essay avowed that liberty never existed in a society that did not keep the powers of government in check.

Another check on government that was necessary for a free government was rotation of office. Because of the corrupt nature of man, the essay argued, people in power must be rotated often to guard against one person acquiring too much power. Power, the essay stated was a "bewitching thing, it too often alter[ed] and vitiate[d] hearts, and by the flattery of food, false friends, and parasites puffs men up to an unnatural size." Therefore, the essay claimed that "a rotation of power and magistracy [were] essentially necessary to a free government."[65]

Bradford addressed the issue further with an essay that paraphrased *Cato's Letters* number 27. The essay began with a summary of Tacitus's reaction to the decline of virtue and liberty toward the end of the Roman Republic. The essay explained that the fall of the Roman Republic was due to the "vice and debauchery" of the leaders, which spread to the people and caused the decline of the society.

Because corruption and other crimes committed by government were not opposed by the people, government "inevitably dwindled into contempt and confusion."[66] The essays warned that if citizens did not judge their leaders and protect their liberty as soon as it was violated, tyranny resulted. "It [was] the duty of every good man," the essay avowed, "to encounter and oppose vice, to discourage immorality, prophaneness, and irreligion, to be resolute in punishing all offenses against the laws of God and their country."[67] Furthermore, people must "encourage the good magistrate in the legal discharge of his duty, and by endeavoring to get men chosen to that trust."[68]

Beginning in 1734, Benjamin Franklin in his *Pennsylvania Gazette* began to print essays that closely resembled some of Trenchard and Gordon's essays. Franklin, however, used the essays differently than Bradford. Franklin synthesized ideas from some of Trenchard and Gordon's works with other writers and created his own work while Bradford usually reprinted essays word for word. Franklin's synthesis usually resulted in a different interpretation of Trenchard and Gordon. For example, Franklin reprinted an essay that resembled *Cato's Letter* number 35 on the subject of public spirit in 1734. Franklin asserted that public spirit was "an earnest desire of the good of the community to which we belong, superior to all other engagements."[69]

Similarly, *Cato's Letters* 35 assured that public spirit was "a passion to promote universal good, with personal pain, loss and peril: It is one man's care for many, and the concern of every man to all."[70] Franklin's essay, however, continued in a very different direction from that of Cato Number 35. Franklin argued that the best form of government was a republic. Franklin believed that a popular government was the best defense against arbitrary governments.[71]

In *Cato's Letters* 85, Trenchard and Gordon explicitly propounded that "liberty may be better preserved by a well poised monarchy, than by any popular government that I know now in the world."[72] Franklin used very similar examples to that of Trenchard and Gordon but he replaced some of the conclusions with his own, which advocated a popular government. On the other hand, Bradford reprinted *Cato's Letters* Number 35 twice but he did not discuss the popular governments as Franklin did.[73]

Franklin reprinted Cato 15 and 38 in the 1730s.[74] These essays discussed the importance of the freedom of speech, the right to judge government officials, liberty, and corruption. Franklin found these subjects favorable, like most printers, because the essays justified their position in society. Printers oftentimes saw themselves as serving the public by informing the public about government, religion, science and any other subject of interest.

Franklin summarized rather than copied essays 15 and 38. Franklin's essay declared that the "freedom of speech is a principal pillar in a free government."[75] He continued that only evil magistrates sought to restrict the freedom of speech. Franklin wrote that the freedom of speech was necessary for the citizens of a country to fulfill their duty to keep government officials in check. *Cato's Letters* 15 and 38 had similar arguments. Cato wrote that the freedom of speech was "a sacred privilege" that was "so essential to free government."[76] Furthermore, Cato stated that "whoever would overthrow the liberty of the nation, must begin by subduing the freedom of speech; a thing terrible to publick traitors."[77]

Franklin summarized *Cato's Letters* 59 on the subject of government in 1736.[78] Cato 59 proclaimed that government should always be administered for the benefit of society. The essay explained the difference between "free" and "arbitrary" governments. In free governments there were checks and restraints placed upon rulers that were expressed in a constitution. In arbitrary governments the prince had unrestrained powers that were never defined.[79] Franklin's essay and Cato essay Number 59 strikingly resemble each other. Franklin's essay began with the statement: "Freedom is the birth-right of every man. We are all born naturally equal." Correspondingly, Cato essay number 59 stated: "All men are born free; liberty is a gift which they receive from God himself." Franklin went on to affirm that a magistrate could not have any power that men did not give them.[80] Similarly, Cato essay 59 wrote, "the right of the magistrate arises only from the right of private men."[81]

Franklin reprinted two paragraphs from Trenchard and Gordon's essay Number 128.[82] Franklin acknowledged that he took part of the essay from the

Cato's Letters collection. The essay addressed a "disaffected laity" and spoke to a "disaffected clergy."[83] The following passage from Cato stated that "the popery came into the Kingdom like a torrent, and arbitrary power appeared undisguised and in the most glaring colors." Franklin then continued by summarizing the rest of the essay. Franklin borrowed the statement that one should "reflect on the Tyranny and persecution our fathers suffered under the Reigns of the Stuarts, and compare them with the Happiness and liberty we enjoy under the present establishment."[84]

The printer of the *Pennsylvania Journal*, William Bradford III, not surprisingly used *Cato's Letters* to argue his political position in a controversy that occurred in the colony in the 1750s. Bradford III was the son of William Bradford, Junior and grandson of the first William Bradford who opened the first printing shop in Philadelphia in 1685. Bradford III was born in New York and moved to Pennsylvania to the house of his uncle, Andrew Bradford of the *American Mercury*, where he was adopted after the death of his father.[85] Andrew Bradford trained Bradford III in the printing trade. Bradford III, therefore, was exposed to what his uncle printed in the *Mercury* in the 1720s and 1730s and this material included many reprintings of *Cato's Letters*.

Bradford III began his own printing shop in 1742 and started the *Pennsylvania Journal or Weekly Advertiser* in December of 1742. *Cato's Letters* were first reprinted in Bradford III's *Pennsylvania Journal* on 23 February 1758, when there was a controversy regarding the powers of the House of Commons over the writ of habeas corpus. On 16 February 1758 the opinion of the House of Commons on the subject of writ of habeas corpus was printed in the *Pennsylvania Journal*. In response an author who called himself "The Watchman" responded by criticizing the House's abuse of power and reprinted *Cato's Letters* 15 on the freedom of speech. The Watchman, quoted directly from Cato, wrote that the "freedom of speech is the great bulwark of Liberty. They prosper and die together."[86] Moreover the essay propounded that "without the freedom of thought, there can be no such thing as wisdom; and without freedom of speech no such thing as public liberty."[87] The essay continued to argue that the freedom of speech was essential to free government and "where a man cannot call his tongue his own he can scarce call anything else his own."[88]

On 9 March 1758 someone wrote a letter to the *Pennsylvania Journal* that directly responded to the Watchman's reprint of Cato 15. First the anonymous letter said the Watchman made a "monstrous disingenuity" to the freedom of speech because of the context of his argument. The anonymous author said the Watchman only reprinted a part of the House of Commons opinion, which misrepresented the House's position. And to add to the insult, the author reprinted a section from *Cato's Letters* 17. The author wrote "the late excellent Mr. Trenchard in one of Cato's essays, say— 'Few men have been desperate enough to attack openly, and barefaced, the liberties of a free people. Such avowed conspirators can rarely succeed: The attempt would destroy itself. . . .'"[89]

The next issue that mentioned Trenchard and Gordon occurred in the *Pennsylvania Journal* on 6 April 1758. A sarcastic letter, written to Humphey Scourge, mentioned Trenchard and Gordon. The letter stated that the British Americans did not have the rights of Britons and further declared that:

> I will teach them to spurn at Magna Charters of privileges and the laws of the English constitution; and if ever I find Locke, Sidney, or *Cato's Letters* within the walls of my jurisdiction, they shall be instantly condemned to flames, their notions of the liberties of the English constitution carefully eradicated and Machiavelli shall be the study of my pupils in their rooms.[90]

The letter most likely was meant to be sarcastic. Most Americans believed that they had the rights of Englishmen. Moreover, most people in the colonies, no matter what their political origination, read and supported Locke, Sidney, and *Cato's Letters*.

Evidence shows that the ideas of Trenchard and Gordon were influential in eighteenth-century Pennsylvania society. They were popular because of the political structure of the colony and the essays in turn encouraged the factious nature of the politics. The way Trenchard and Gordon's essays were used also encouraged the development of a liberal interpretation of speech and press freedom and expanded the public sphere in Pennsylvania. Evidence also suggests that Trenchard and Gordon's works were well integrated into the consciousness of many Pennsylvanians—Quakers, Anglicans, Germans, and proprietary supporters.

Pennsylvanians also changed the meaning of Trenchard and Gordon's ideas involving the freedom of speech and the right to judge government officials. Pennsylvanians reprinted Cato's essays on the freedom of speech and the duty to judge government officials to persuade freeholders that they were the ones who should judge government officials to keep their power in check. Trenchard and Gordon, however, did not intend for everyone to judge government officials. Instead, Trenchard and Gordon believed that only economically and politically independent citizens were supposed to judge government officials, not just anyone.[91]

Because Trenchard and Gordon entered into local political controversies, many Pennsylvanians knew *of* Trenchard and Gordon. What they knew of Trenchard and Gordon probably was from newspapers, which only reprinted select parts of their works. Pennsylvania newspaper readers had a much different idea of what Trenchard and Gordon advocated by the way their essays were reprinted.

From 1720 to 1760 the attempt by politicians to encourage people to become involved in politics resulted in the development of a new political culture. In Pennsylvania, the publishing of political literature placed a notable amount of importance on the press because newspapers made it possible for politicians to inform the populace when desired. Since select essays written by Trenchard and Gordon supported the involvement of people in politics and were reprinted numerous times in Pennsylvania, their essays reinforced a new political culture in the colony. This new political culture allowed many people traditionally outside the elite voting community to practice active citizenship by becoming involved in political controversies.

NOTES

1. Yet there were brief periods when newspapers did not reprint their works. For example, in the 1740s printers failed to reprint their essays in their newspapers. However, one of the newspaper printers, Andrew Bradford, printed the entire *Independent Whig* collection in 1740. Moreover, Trenchard and Gordon's works were advertised throughout the 1740s in most of the newspapers.

2. Gary Nash. "The Transformation of Urban Politics 1700–1765," *The Journal of American History*, Volume 60, Issue 3 (December 1973), 605–632.

3. Nash, "The Transformation of Urban Politics 1700–1765," 607.

4. This is the same Andrew Hamilton who defended John Peter Zenger in New York in 1735. See Chapter 4.

5. After William Penn died in 1718, there were fourteen years of uncertainty in Penn's family about who owned the land. Penn's three sons from his second wife, John, Thomas, and Richard inherited the colony of Pennsylvania. The offspring from Penn's first marriage, the Springett side of the family, however, questioned the validity of Penn's will. The controversy continued for many years. See Alan Tully, *Forming American Politics: Ideals, Interests, and Institutions in Colonial New York and Pennsylvania* (Baltimore: The Johns Hopkins University Press, 1994), 3–5.

6. Tully, *Forming American Politics*, 15–17.

7. Nash, "The Transformation of Urban Politics 1700–1765," 606.

8. William Bradford defended himself and argued that the tracts he published were not seditious against the government; he was just exercising freedom of conscience. Bradford elaborated further and said that it was "not sedition, but wholly relating to a religious difference." Therefore, the tracts did not set out to defame the government or undermine the establishment; they only advocated a religious difference. The jury was split and Bradford was released. Bradford decided to leave Pennsylvania after he received strict orders not to print anything without prior approval by the Society of Friends. Bradford moved to New York and opened a printing shop and eventually founded the *New York Gazette* in 1725. See William Robert Shepherd, *History of Proprietary Government in Pennsylvania* (New York: AMS Press, Inc., 1967), 273.The *Mercury* was very popular throughout the colonies for more than ten years. Bradford

shipped newspapers to New York where his father would sell them. Bradford also had agreements with several other printing shops to distribute the *Mercury*. Bradford made deals with printers in Rhode Island, Massachusetts, Virginia, and with New York printers other than his father. Furthermore, Bradford held the position of postmaster, which allowed him to send his newspapers for free. See Anna Janney DeArmond, *Andrew Bradford: Colonial Journalist* (New York: Greenwood Press, 1969), 219. Andrew was the son of William Bradford, who moved from Britain to Pennsylvania in 1685. William Bradford owned and operated a printing press in Pennsylvania. In 1692 William Bradford involved himself in printing controversial religious tracts for George Keith, who was an itinerant Quaker preacher. Keith emphasized the need for more structure in the church leadership and he advocated a greater reliance on scripture as authority rather than just the "inner light." Keith's tracts horrified some of the Quakers, and the Quaker government blamed Bradford for printing the alleged heresy. The Quaker officials charged Bradford with seditious libel. Bradford was subsequently arrested and his printing press seized.

9. Frederick B. Tolles, *Meeting House and County House: The Quaker Merchants of Colonial Philadelphia, 1682–1763* (New York: University of North Carolina Press, 1948; reprint, New York: W. W. Norton & Company, 1963), 100–106. Wealthy conservative Quakers who objected to the paper money scheme included Isaac Norris, James Logan, and Richard Hill. Debtors favored inflation because inflation allowed them to pay back their debts with less valuable money. The loaner always tried to limit inflation.

10. Gary Nash, *Quakers and Politics: Pennsylvania, 1681–1726* (Princeton, NJ: Princeton University Press, 1968), 330–335. Nash asserted that all segments of society clamored for the paper currency plan except the wealthiest merchants, 333.

11. *American Weekly Mercury*, 2 January 1721/22.

12. DeArmond, *Andrew Bradford*, 13–15. See William David and Julie Hedgepeth Williams, *The Early American Press, 1690–1783* (Westport, CT: Greenwood Press, 1994), 57. They argued that it was plausible that Bradford was not aware of the pamphlet and the comment in his *Mercury* because he was personally against the issuance of paper money due to his sympathies for the proprietary party.

13. DeArmond, *Andrew Bradford*, 14–15.

14. Sloan and Williams argued that Bradford did not publish information because of political reasons. They argue that Bradford was a businessman and only published "the news" and left his political and religious sentiments in the background. See pp 53–56. However, I disagree with their synopsis. Bradford reprinted *Cato's Letters* at particular times and addressed issues very similar to the events happening in the colony or elsewhere that caught the attention of Bradford. There is a possibility that it was a coincidence.

15. Trenchard and Gordon began their *Cato's Letters* series after the South-Sea Bubble crisis caused an economic panic in England. Trenchard and Gordon wrote more than a dozen essays criticizing the government for its role in the crisis and asserting against any further government action to help bail out the company. The ironic part of this scene was that Bradford was using select essays from *Cato's Letters* to advocate the opposite position. Bradford was trying to get the provincial government involved in the economy to help alleviate the financial crisis in Pennsylvania.

16. *AWM*, 13 February–20 February 1722. *Cato's Letters*, Number 38. "The Right and Capacity of the People to judge of Government."
17. *AWM*, 13 February–20 February 1722.
18. AWM, 13 February–20 February 1722.
19. *AWM*, 10 March–15 March 1722. *Cato's Letters*, Number 40. "Considerations on the Restless and Selfish Spirit of Man."
20. *AWM*, 10 March–15 March 1722. *Cato's Letters*, Number 40.
21. *AWM*, 14–21 June 1722. *Cato's Letters*, Number 33. "Cautions against the natural encroachment of power."
22. Trenchard and Gordon would have disagreed with the way Bradford used their essay. Trenchard and Gordon believed in a balanced government with an aristocracy and not a democratic form that Bradford was advocating.
23. *AWM*, 14–21 June 1722. *Cato's Letters*, Number 33. "Cautions against the natural encroachment of power." This essay is based on John Locke's theories on government.
24. *AWM*, 14–21 June 1722. *Cato's Letters*, Number 33.
25. *AWM*, 14–21 June 1722. *Cato's Letters*, Number 33.
26. Most people in eighteenth-century England and British North America believed political parties or factions were dangerous to British liberty.
27. *AWM*, 31 December–7 January 1723. *Cato's Letters*, Number 131 "Of Reverence true and false."
28. *AWM*, 12–19 April 1722. *Cato's Letters*, Number 35. "Of Public Spirit."
29. *AWM*, 12–19 April 1722. *Cato's Letters*, Number 35.
30. The *American Weekly Mercury* added the emphasis to this word. It may have been underlined in the original printing of the letter in the *London Journal*. However, it is not emphasized in the volume set but other words throughout the text were emphasized.
31. *AWM*, 4–11 February 1724 and then on 11–18 February 1724. *Cato's Letters*, Numbers 128 and 130 "Address to such of the Laity as are followers of the disaffected clergy, and of their accomplices" and "The same address continued."
32. *AWM*, 12–19 April 1722. *Cato's Letters*, Number 35. "Of Public Spirit."
33. *AWM*, 22–29March 1722. *Cato's Letters*, Number 34. "Of Flattery."
34. Trenchard and Gordon considered the "Court" to be the people in power. Bradford probably meant the same thing.
35. *AWM*, 31 May–7 June 1722. *Cato's Letters*, Number 36. "Of Loyalty."
36. *AWM*, 31 December–7 January 1723. *Cato's Letters*, Number 131. "Of Reverence true and false."
37. Hannah Penn, who was William's second wife, appointed Patrick Gordon. See DeArmond, 89.
38. It is unknown why the disagreement occurred.
39. DeArmond and Sloan and Williams all found that the dispute between Hamilton and Gordon had something to do with a fight between their children. It is unknown what about but apparently it was serious enough to cause a great political battle. DeArmond, 88–89. Sloan and Williams.
40. *The Pennsylvania Gazette* was formed out of Samuel Keimer's newspaper titled the *Universal Instructor in all Arts and Sciences: and Pennsylvania Gazette* in 1729.

Benjamin Franklin had worked for Samuel Keimer but they departed on bad terms. For more information on Keimer see Stephen Bloore, "Samuel Keimer: A Footnote to the Life of Franklin," *The Pennsylvania Magazine of History and Biography* (Philadelphia: The Historical Society of Pennsylvania, 1930) Vol. LIV pp. 255–287.

41. Benjamin Franklin's *Pennsylvania Gazette* rivaled Bradford's *Mercury*; however, sometimes they had common interests. Franklin agreed with Bradford's support for the issuance of the paper currency in Pennsylvania. He, too, believed it would help alleviate the economic recession of the colony. Franklin's newspaper also opposed much of the proprietor's policies but he was also against some of the Quakers' positions, such as their pacifism stance. In the late 1720s, Franklin used his *Gazette* to support Andrew Hamilton, and Bradford used his power to oppose Hamilton vehemently. Yet, both Franklin and Bradford reprinted essays from Trenchard and Gordon's *Cato's Letters* series.

42. See Chapter 4.

43. These very same ideas were used in Andrew Hamilton's opening in the defense of Zenger six years later.

44. *AWM*, 5–12 March 1733–34. Number 741. *Cato's Letters*, Number 15.

45. *AWM*, 5–12 March 1733–34. Number 741.

46. *AWM*, 5–12 March 1733–34. Number 741. *Cato's Letters*, Number 15.

47. *AWM*, 5–12 March 1733–34. Number 741. *Cato's Letters*, Number 15.

48. *AWM*, 10–17April 1728/29. Number 484. *Cato's Letters*, Number 102.

49. The Busy-Body series was a collection of essays that were written by Joseph Breintnall and later Benjamin Franklin wrote several of the essays. According to Sloan and DeArmond, Franklin authored the first couple of the Busy-Body series and Joseph Breintnall authored the remaining numbers including the most controversial numbers (Numbers 31 and 32).

50. *AWM*, 11–18 September 1729. Number 473. *Cato's Letters*, Number 39.

51. *AWM*, 11–18 September 1729. Number 473. *Cato's Letters*, Number 39.

52. DeArmond, *Andrew Bradford*, 18. The imprisonment could not have been for very long.

53. *AWM*, 18–25 September 1729. *Cato's Letters*, Numbers 69 and 70.

54. See Chapter 4.

55. *AWM*, 27 September 1733.

56. *AWM*, 20–27 September 1733. Number 717. *Cato's Letters*, Number 38.

57. *AWM*, 27 September–4 October 1733. Number 718.

58. *AWM*, 27 September–4 October 1733. Number 718.

59. *AWM* ,27 September–4 October 1733. Number 718.

60. Tully, *Forming America Politics*, 79–82.

61. *AWM*, 2–9 April 1730. *Cato's Letters*, Number 45.

62. *AWM*, 7–14 May 1730. *Cato's Letters*, Number 123.

63. *AWM*, 21 May 1730. *Cato's Letters*, Number 124.

64. *AWM*, 27 April–4 May 1738. *Cato's Letters*, Numbers 38 and 61.

65. *AWM*, 27 April–4 May 1738. *Cato's Letters*, Numbers 38 and 61.

66. *AWM*, 27 April–4 May 1738. *Cato's Letters*, Numbers 38 and 61.

67. *AWM*, 27 April–4 May 1738. *Cato's Letters*, Numbers 38 and 61.

68. *AWM*, 27 April–4 May 1738. *Cato's Letters*, Numbers 38 and 61.

69. *Pennsylvania Gazette*, 15–22 August 1734.
70. *Cato's Letters*, Number 35.
71. *Pennsylvania Gazette*, 15–22 August 1734.
72. *Cato's Letters*, Number 85.
73. *Cato's Letters*, Number 35 was reprinted in the *American Weekly Mercury* on 12 April 1722 and 13 April 1738.
74. *Cato's Letters*, Number 15 was reprinted in the *American Weekly Mercury* on 5 March 1734 and Number 38 was reprinted on 13 February 1722, 20 September 1734, 27 April 1738. The *Pennsylvania Gazette* summarized *Cato's Letters*, Number 15 on 10 November 1737 and Number 38 on 10 November 1737, 1 December 1737, and 11 May 1738.
75. *Cato's Letters*, Number 15.
76. *Cato's Letters*, Numbers 15 and 38.
77. *Cato's Letters*, Number 15.
78. The *American Weekly Mercury* reprinted *Cato's Letters*, Number 59 on 30 March 1732 and the *Pennsylvania Gazette* reprinted Number 59 on 8 April 1736.
79. *AWM*, 30 March-6 April 1732. Number 640 *Cato's Letters*, Number 59.
80. *Pennsylvania Gazette*, 3–10 June 1736.
81. *Cato's Letters*, Number 59.
82. *Pennsylvania Gazette*, 3–10 June 1736. *Cato's Letters*, Number 128. Bradford reprinted this essay in the *American Weekly Mercury* in 1724.
83. *Pennsylvania Gazette*, 3–10 June 1736.
84. *Pennsylvania Gazette*, 3–10 June 1736.
85. Thomas, *History of Printing in America*, 240–243.
86. *Pennsylvania Journal and Weekly Advertiser*, 23 February 1758. *Cato's Letters*, Number 15.
87. *Pennsylvania Journal and Weekly Advertiser*, 23 February 1758. *Cato's Letters*, Number 15.
88. *Pennsylvania Journal and Weekly Advertiser*, 23 February 1758. *Cato's Letters*, Number 15.
89. *Pennsylvania Journal and Weekly Advertiser*, 9 March 1758. *Cato's Letters*, Number 17.
90. *Pennsylvania Journal*, 6 April 1758.
91. *Cato's Letters*, Numbers 8, 13, 19, 27, 31, 40, 43–45, 49, 51–52, 57, 82, 85, 105, 115, 117, 123, 134.

Chapter Six

Trenchard and Gordon's Works in British North American Colonial Newspapers After 1760

Trenchard and Gordon's works were reprinted during the 1760s and 1770s in British America. A select number of essays from the *Cato's Letters* series were reprinted in newspapers throughout the colonies. Their works were no longer limited to newspapers in the urban areas of New York City, Philadelphia, and Boston. After 1760, Trenchard and Gordon's essays were also reprinted in the press in Virginia, Georgia, Maryland, Rhode Island, and Connecticut. The most widespread pieces of *Cato's Letters* were reprinted as part of John Dickinson's series, *Letters From a Farmer in Pennsylvania*. More than 80% of the English newspapers in the North American colonies reprinted Dickinson's essays.[1] In addition, the Dickinson essays were reprinted in pamphlet form in Philadelphia, Boston, New York, and Williamsburg.[2] Dickinson's essays helped disseminate a few select ideas from Cato to a large percentage of the populace in the 1760s and 1770s.

Selections from Trenchard and Gordon's works appeared in opposition newspapers in Massachusetts, New York, and Pennsylvania after the 1760s, as they did during controversies earlier in the century. In response to the enforcement and rise of colonial taxes by Parliament, opposition newspapers printed essays objecting to the policies. Some of the opposition essays reprinted selections from Trenchard and Gordon's works.

A Boston opposition newspaper, the *Massachusetts Spy*, responded to Parliament's policies by reprinting essays from *Cato's Letters*. The printer, Isaiah Thomas, began the *Massachusetts Spy* in March of 1771.[3] Thomas began the *Spy* with the supposed intent to create a nonpartisan newspaper that would allow both Whigs and Tories to publish information.[4] Due to this goal, Thomas used several essays from Trenchard and Gordon to support the freedom of speech. Five of the nine essays reprinted in the *Spy* discussed the significance of speech freedom in free societies. *Cato's Letters* number 15, "Of Freedom of Speech: That the same is inseparable from public Liberty," was reprinted three times in 1771 in the *Spy*. In addition, *Cato's Letters* 100 and 101, which also discussed speech freedom were reprinted. Because of the controversial British policies, Thomas found it impossible to maintain the *Massachusetts Spy* as a nonpartisan newspaper. The *Massachusetts Spy* became a voice for the Whig interests by November 1771.[5]

After the *Massachusetts Spy* became a partisan newspaper, Thomas reprinted three essays by Trenchard and Gordon. Thomas reprinted *Cato's Letters* 113, "Letter to Cato, concerning his many Adversaries and Answerers." This essay, which explained how oftentimes people decided to oppose someone for inappropriate reasons, fit well with Thomas's situation in November of 1771. Thomas had just printed an essay in the *Spy* under the pseudonym Mucius Scaevola that apparently offended Governor Hutchinson.[6]

Thomas was called before the Council on several occasions, and he refused to appear. During the conflict, Thomas thought it would be appropriate to reprint *Cato's Letters* 112 on the subject of liberty.[7] Cato asserted that government officials who were truly "friends of public liberty" were "the only true lovers of prosperity."[8]

The last Trenchard and Gordon essay to appear in the *Massachusetts Spy* was printed in 1773. This essay discussed Brutus from antiquity, and how honorable he was because he was virtuous and favored public liberty.[9] This essay could be perceived as an affront to the governor and/or the various controversial British taxes being passed at the time. Thomas continued to print his *Spy* even after British occupation of Boston.[10]

Typical of opposition press in New York, John Holt, the printer of the *New York Journal or General Advertiser* (*NYJ*), reprinted twelve essays that borrowed from *Cato's Letters*. According to historian Isaiah Thomas, "Holt was a man of ardent feeling, and a high churchman, but a firm whig, a good writer, and a warm advocate of the cause of his country."[11] With Holt's political orientation, it made sense that he reprinted some of Trenchard and Gordon's works during this time of controversy in New York.

The events of the 1760s led essay writers of the *NYJ* to use Trenchard and Gordon's rhetoric to protest against the perceived encroachments of the colonists' rights. The *NYJ* was a publication created to direct popular opposition against England's policies toward the colonies. However, this time Trenchard and Gordon's essays were not simply reprinted; instead, the essays in the *NYJ* borrowed small sections from individual essays. The *NYJ* printed select sections from essays that discussed freedom of speech, the right to judge government officials, the danger of standing armies, and corruption and the danger it had on free societies. These essays directly addressed the disputes colonists had with royal governors and imperial England.

The first series of Cato's essays to appear in the *NYJ* occurred in response to George Grenville's policies, which began in 1763.[12] Grenville increased the standing army present in the American colonies and the program required the colonists to pay for the maintenance of the army. Grenville also sought to stop colonists from evasion of trade laws. Grenville first attempted to enforce existing trade regulations, and then he placed more taxes on the colonists to raise revenue. The colonists reacted to Grenville's program in various ways.

Holt of the *NYJ* decided to print an essay that summarized two of Cato's essays. The essay on 11 December 1766 resembled *Cato's Letters* 60 and 62. All three of the essays avowed that the people must be consulted when levying taxes. The essay stated "without all their consents, [meaning the Crown, House of Lords, and House of Commons or their equivalent] no law can be made, nor a penny of money levied upon the subjects."[13] The *NYJ* essay then reminded the reader of the importance of a balanced government, which was necessary to keep government free from arbitrary rule.

The *NYJ* borrowed several lines from Trenchard and Gordon regarding the danger of standing armies. Many colonists opposed the American Mutiny Act of 1765, known by the colonists as the Quartering Act. This act required colonists to provide barracks and supplies for British soldiers. The *NYJ* borrowed several lines from Trenchard and Gordon regarding the danger of standing armies. On 24 December 1766, the *NYJ* printed an essay on the importance of militias, which were defined as citizen armies rather than professional armies.[14]

On 6 October 1774, the *NYJ* again published a letter that attacked the use of a standing army in peacetime. The essay reiterated the arguments of *Cato's Letters* 94 and 95. Trenchard and Gordon and the author of the *NYJ* essay considered the standing army "the most dangerous enemy to the liberties of a nation that can be thought of."[5] The essay continued: "No prince, no minister, has ever made an attempt upon the rights of a people, until he found himself at the head of an army to put his enterprise into execution."[6] The author concurred with Trenchard's arguments that a well-regulated militia was the best defense against aggressors—foreign and domestic.[7] Only two essays of *Cato's Letters* addressed the issue of standing armies, but this subject was so important to New Yorkers that they chose to emphasize their concern by overstating Trenchard and Gordon's arguments.

Cato number 15, regarding the freedom of speech, appeared in the *NYJ* several times to protest British policies. This essay asserted that the press had a crucial role in society because it brought important information to the public. The author believed that for the most part printers supported the public good. The essay further argued that the press provided citizens with important information and consequently helped citizens perform their duty to judge government officials.[18]

Again Cato 15 was reprinted but this time it was noted that the essay was taken third hand from the *Boston Gazette*. The famous statement made in Cato 15 was included and it read: "Freedom of Speech is the great Bulwark of Liberty; they prosper and die together."[19] The essay borrowed only a few of the paragraphs from the essay, but the author was sure to include sections that had the most fervent rhetoric.

Speech freedom was also the subject of an essay after Alexander McDougall was jailed for publishing a provocative pamphlet against the New York Assembly.[20] Again the *NYJ* reprinted *Cato's Letters* 15 on the freedom of speech and also included quotes from the *Craftsman* regarding the freedom of press.[21] In addition to reprinting number 15, Holt reprinted the transcript from the John Peter Zenger Trial, which was based on *Cato's Letters* 38. The article emphasized the argument that citizens had a duty to judge government officials. Directly connected to this duty was the need for a free press.[22]

The *NYJ* also published an essay that apparently borrowed several passages from *Cato's Letters* 18 and 26. The article contended that luxury was the "bane of liberty, virtue, prosperity, and every blessing that can be greatly precious to a community."[23] The essay further testified that human nature was corrupt and ministers that were allowed to rule by corrupt means must be stopped. Therefore, government must check and restrain luxury. Cato number 18 argued similarly and claimed that public corruption had the ability to ruin a state. In addition, Cato 26 also addressed the negative effects of corruption on a society.[24]

On 12 July 1770 an article appeared that mentioned Cato. The article said: "Get up ye lazy citizens and listen to the patriotic Cato." The essay did not quote from the *Cato's Letters* series. Instead the essay directly attacked specific government policies placed on the colonists. The article's "Cato" could have been referring to Addison's Cato or the Roman Cato. The style and tone of the essay that followed the quote, however, resembled that of Trenchard and Gordon's Cato character.[25]

The last reprinting of Trenchard and Gordon's works in the colony of New York occurred on 20 October 1774. Cato essay 33 was printed second hand from the *Morning Chronicle*. The primary theme of the essay was that because it was human nature to acquire as much power as possible, there must be checks on all positions of power. The author, Brutus, concluded with Cato's direct words: "Power without control belongs to God alone; and no man ought to be trusted with what no man is equal to."[26]

Even though only select ideas from *Cato's Letters* were reprinted, the limited arguments had a profound influence on the reading public, because the controversy between imperial England and the colonies was intensifying year by year. Most of Trenchard and Gordon's essays, however, were not reprinted in their entirety. Instead, only small paraphrased sections were used. In addition, the essays appearing in the 1760s often failed to acknowledge where the ideas originated. This development was significant because it reflected how a "New York" Trenchard and Gordon developed. Colonists no longer saw the oppositional discourse as Trenchard and Gordon but rather as their own.

In response to some new tax legislation instituted by Parliament, Trenchard and Gordon's works appeared in a Pennsylvania newspaper. A Philadelphia newspaper, the *Pennsylvania Journal*, responded to the raising of taxes by reprinting a Trenchard and Gordon essay that addressed taxation.

On 5 April 1764, England raised duties on many American products including sugar and also made duties and fines payable only in sterling. In addition, the Currency Act was passed on 19 April 1764, which prohibited paper money in colonies south of New York meaning all paper money in circulation was to be withdrawn.[27]

The essay asserted that "if, in taxing labor and manufacturers, we exceed a certain proportion, we discourage industry; and destroy that labor and those manufactures."[28] The essay further complained that "when higher duties are laid, the product is not increased; but the trade is lost, or the goods are run."[29] The newspaper dared to continue with Cato's essay which stated that high taxes produce only "bitterness, murmuring, universal discontent and their end, generally *Rebellion* [emphasis added in the *Journal*]...."[30]

On 17 August 1769, Bradford III reprinted *Cato's Letters* 97 titled "How Much it is the interest of Governors to use the Governed well; with an Enquiry into the Causes of Disaffection in England." The essay fit well into the political climate of the colonies during this time. The essay contended that governments that were "founded upon oppression" always found it necessary to take "away all the means of self-defense from those who have more right to use them."[31] In contrast, the essay argued that when a government was "founded upon liberty and equal laws" a leader must govern justly or else the people would not support him. "Wise governors," therefore, would not exorbitantly raise taxes above what the public could afford. Furthermore, governors in "free" countries would not use funds for unpopular reasons.[32] This essay seemed to be directed against the Mutiny/Quartering Act that obliged colonists to provide barracks and supplies for British soldiers. In order to support the troops, taxes had to be raised and taxes were very unpopular in the British colonies.

Twice Bradford III mentioned Cato 15 and 38 when he referred to the John Peter Zenger Trial from 1733, in the *Pennsylvania Journal*.[33] The essays and articles maintained that wherever truth was "dangerous," liberty was "precarious."[34] The essays continued: "government [was] nothing but a trust, committed by the people, or the majority of them, to one or a few, who are to attend upon affairs of all...." This "trust", furthermore, must be "bounded with many and strong restraints."[35]

The essays also asserted that statesmen who looked out for the "public good" should be rewarded, but if a ruler sought only his own interests, he should be punished. The people, therefore, had to keep watch over their statesmen and judge their actions. The essay further argued that it was not only a right for citizens to judge their rulers, it was a duty that they watch over their officials. The essay ended with a prolific statement:

> By the Bill of Rights [Declaration of Rights 1689] and the Act of Settlement, at the Revolution [1688]; a right is asserted to the people applying to the King and to the Parliament, by petition and address, for a redress of public grievances and mismanagement, when such there are, of which they are left to judge; and the difference between free and enslaved countries lies principally here, that in the former, their magistrates must consult the voice and interest of the people; but in the latter, the private will, interest, and pleasure of the governors, are the sole end and motives of their administration.[36]

The author of the essay and article in the *Pennsylvania Journal* contended that it was the right of every British citizen to judge government officials. By using *Cato's Letters* to argue the point, it showed how colonists viewed their response to British policy—completely within their rights as British citizens.

The last mention of Cato in Bradford's newspaper appeared on 6 July 1774 and 19 January 1774. The two essays were signed Cato; however, they were not pirated directly from Trenchard and Gordon's series. Nonetheless, the two journal essays called the citizens of the colonies to rise up against their "oppressors" and this argument correlated to Cato's reprinting of Algernon Sidney's essay titled "Character of a good and an evil Magistrate." This reprinted essay written by Sidney advocated the "right" of citizens to rise up against unjust rulers.[37] Furthermore, the essay asserted that the citizens of the country must rise up against "these unconstitutional commissioners."[38]

Bradford III continued to print the *Pennsylvania Journal* until the British occupied Philadelphia in September 1777. The newspaper resumed after the war until 18 September 1793 under his son, Thomas. Trenchard and Gordon's works, however, were not reprinted, summarized or quoted after 1774.

The protest movement against British tax policies in the 1760s led the printer of the *Pennsylvania Chronicle and Universal Advertiser,* William Goddard, to print essays by John Dickinson that summarized some of Trenchard and Gordon's essays. Goddard, in partnership with two leading Pennsylvania citizens, Joseph Galloway and Thomas Wharton, first published the newspaper on 26 January 1767.[39] According to historian Isaiah Thomas, the *Chronicle* seemed to be impartial until Goddard printed Dickinson's series the *Farmer's Letters*.

The *Chronicle* published Dickinson's twelve-essay series before any other paper. Then other newspapers reprinted the series throughout the late 1760s and early 1770s. Many of the newspapers were long-lasting established papers, not just opposition papers. Newspapers such as the *Georgia Gazette, Virginia Gazette, Maryland Gazette,* and *Connecticut Gazette,* also eventually reprinted some of Cato's essays indirectly through Dickinson. It was Dickinson and his conservative use of a select number of *Cato's Letters* that enticed these colonial printers to reprint Trenchard and Gordon's ideas and become part of opposition political culture that already existed in Massachusetts, New York, and Pennsylvania.

John Dickinson was born in Maryland in 1732 and grew up and received an education in Delaware.[40] He went to London to study law and went to Pennsylvania to practice law. In 1760 he was admitted to the Assembly of Delaware and then the Assembly of Pennsylvania.

In response to English policies, Dickinson wrote a series of essays that addressed the events that occurred in the colonies during the late 1760s. He signed his essays *Letters From a Farmer in Pennsylvania,* even though he was not a Pennsylvanian or a farmer. Dickinson elaborated on how the policies of England were a threat to liberty, the unfair taxes on colonies, the fear of political corruption, and the threat of the standing army in the colonies.[41] Trenchard and Gordon's *Cato's Letters* addressed these same issues. Dickinson integrated the ideas of Trenchard and Gordon with his own; he did not simply copy Trenchard and Gordon's essays.

The first letter which appeared on 30 November 1767, addressed the British policies placed upon the colonies in North America specifically commenting on the "unjust" Stamp Act.[42] Farmer letter number two pulled from *Cato's Letters* 106 titled "Of Plantations and Colonies," and Cato 10 on taxes.[43] The essay declared that taxes were to "regulate trade, and preserve or promote a mutually beneficial intercourse between the several constituent parts of the empire . . . and thus to promote the general welfare."[44]

Dickinson's letter V also quoted directly from *Cato's Letters* 106. The essays propounded that there were two ways to stop a colony from "throwing off their dependence," which included using force or "using them well."[45] To use force to keep colonies dependent required a standing army and often resulted in failure, stated the authors. Moreover, the use of force costs too much; since the "mother" country would have to pay continually to keep the colony under control. In contrast, if the mother country treated her colonies well, the colonies would not see the need to become independent. The essay further advocated that the mother country always tried to keep colonies dependent and it was more "effectually done by gentle and sensible methods, than by power alone."[46]

Dickinson's essay number VI summarized *Cato's Letters* 38. Dickinson asked: "Ought not the people therefore to watch? To observe facts? To search into causes? To Investigate designs? And have they not a right of Judging from the evidence before them, on no slighter points than their liberty and happiness?" Cato essay 38 advocated the same idea; that it was in the best interest for citizens to judge government officials in order to protect their liberty.[47]

Dickinson's essay number IX briefly protested against the presence of the standing army in the colonies. He especially noted the absurdity that the colonists had to pay for the maintenance of the army, which was allegedly suppressing them. Dickinson's main point that the standing army was a threat to liberty also was addressed in *Cato's Letters* number 125 on standing armies. Dickinson, however, did not quote directly from the Cato collection.[48]

Farmer's Letter number XI and *Cato's Letters* 70 had striking similarities. Both Cato and Dickinson elaborated on the need to guard against men who encroached upon other people's liberty. Both essays also stated that mixed government helped to check governors. Dickinson's number XI essay resembled Cato 125 on the subject of standing armies. Dickinson argued that "a standing army and excise [tax] have . . . always [been] hated, always feared, always opposed, at length swelled up to their vast present bulk." In *Cato's Letters* 125, Trenchard and Gordon asserted a similar point. They protested against standing armies and taxes and believed they were the roots of evil and corruption. Moreover, "a government begun by armies, and the violation of property, must be continued by armies, oppression and violence."[49]

With his essays, Dickinson encouraged people to become involved in politics of the 1760s. He tried to show that the policies of the metropolis were not just, and that their British liberties were in danger. By using ideas from *Cato's Letters*, he explained to colonists how urgent his message was and how important it was for colonists to stand up for their rights. For a Pennsylvanian, using ideas from Cato was logical since their works were well known by many newspaper readers. The shift in importance was the fact that newspapers that traditionally did not use such opposition literature reprinted Dickinson's essays, and therefore indirectly used some of Cato's essays.

Since Dickinson borrowed sections from only five of Trenchard and Gordon's essays, colonists had a limited understanding of what *Cato's Letters* advocated. The message that Dickinson sent from Trenchard and Gordon was that they deplored taxes, wanted the right to judge government officials, were against standing armies, and wanted to be treated with respect as colonists. These ideas from Cato were very limited compared to what colonists in urban areas read of Cato before the 1760s.

Nevertheless, the use of *Cato's Letters* during the 1760s and 1770s had great influence on the reading public because the controversy between England and the colonies had captured many people's attention. Most of Trenchard and Gordon's works, however, were not reprinted in their entirety in this era. Instead, only small paraphrased sections were used. In fact, the essays that appeared in the 1760s many times failed to acknowledge that the ideas came from Trenchard and Gordon. This change is significant because it reflects how Trenchard and Gordon's ideas were becoming part of the colonists' vocabulary, and colonists no longer saw the ideas as Cato's but rather as their own.

NOTES

1. Out of the 23 English newspapers, 19 of them reprinted John Dickinson's *Farmer's Letters* series. See Carl F. Kaestle's article "The Public Reaction to John Dickinson's Farmer's Letters." *Proceedings of the American Antiquarian Society* Volume 78 (Worcester, MA: Society of American Antiquarian, 1969), 351.

2. Carl F. Kaestle, "The Public Reaction to John Dickinson's Farmer's Letter," *Proceedings of the American Antiquarian Society* 78, pt. 2 (1969): 323–353.

3. Isaiah Thomas, *The History of Printing in America: With a Biography of Printers & an Account of Newspapers* (New York: Weathervane Books, 1970), 154–170. Isaiah Thomas and business partner Zechariah Fowle began publishing a newspaper titled: *The Massachusetts Spy* but it was discontinued in December of 1770. Then on 5 March 1771, Thomas began another paper with the same title: *The Massachusetts Spy*.

4. The two parties, Whigs and Tories, were named during this period. The Whigs were the supporters of what they considered American liberty and the Tories supported British policies.

5. Thomas, *The History of Printing in America*, 164–165.

6. The *Massachusetts Spy*, November 1771. *Cato's Letters,* Number 113.

7. The *Massachusetts Spy*, 19 December 1771. *Cato's Letters,* Number 112.

8. *Cato's Letters,* Number 112.

9. The *Massachusetts Spy*, 13 May 1773. *Cato's Letters,* Number 23.

10. Thomas moved his press to Worcester and printed the *Spy* from there, after the British occupation of Boston.

11. Thomas, *The History of Printing in America*, 303–304.

12. Grenville's policies were not new—most of them began under the Bute ministry including the presence of a standing army in the American colonies and "the crucial public commitment to finance it by a colonial tax." Peter Thomas, "The Grenville Program, 1763–1765," in Greene and Pole, 111.

13. *New York Journal*, 11 December 1766. *Cato's Letters*, Numbers 60 and 62.

14. *New York Journal*, 24 December 1766. *Cato's Letters,* Number 65.

15. *New York Journal*, 6 October 1774. *Cato's Letters,* Numbers 94 and 95.

16. *New York Journal*, 6 October 1774. *Cato's Letters,* Numbers 94 and 95.

17. *New York Journal*, 6 October 1774. *Cato's Letters,* Numbers 94 and 95.

18. *New York Journal,* 19 March 1767. *Cato's Letters*, Number 15.

19. *New York Journal,* 19 March 1767. *Cato's Letters*, Number 15.

20. For more information on Alexander McDougall see Michael Kammen. *Colonial New York: A History*. New York: Charles Scribner's Sons, 1975.

21. *New York Journal*, 21 February 1771. *Cato's Letters*, Number 15.
22. *New York Journal*, 29 March 1770. *Cato's Letters*, Number 38.
23. *New York Journal*, 9 April 1767. *Cato's Letters*, Numbers 18 and 26.
24. *New York Journal*, 9 April 1767. *Cato's Letters*, Numbers 18 and 26.
25. *New York Journal*, 12 July 1770.
26. *New York Journal*, 20 October 1774. *Cato's Letters*, Number 33.
27. For more information on what events occurred in the 1760s see Jack P. Greene and J. R. Pole's *The Blackwell Encyclopedia of the American Revolution*. Cambridge, MA: Blackwell Publishers, 1991.
28. *Pennsylvania Journal*, 28 June 1764. *Cato's Letters*, Number 10.
29. *Pennsylvania Journal*, 28 June 1764. *Cato's Letters*, Number 10.
30. *Pennsylvania Journal*, 28 June 1764. *Cato's Letters*, Number 10.
31. *Pennsylvania Journal*, 17 August 1769 and *Cato's Letters*, Number 97.
32. *Pennsylvania Journal*, 17 August 1769 and *Cato's Letters*, Number 97.
33. See Chapter 4.
34. *Pennsylvania Journal*, 15 March 1770 and 26 May 1773.
35. *Pennsylvania Journal*, 15 March 1770 and 26 May 1773.
36. *Pennsylvania Journal*, 26 May 1773. *Cato's Letters*, Number 38.
37. *Cato's Letters* Number 37. Also *Cato's Letters*, Number 56 advocated the right of citizens to rise up against tyrants. Cato Number 56 titled "A Vindication of Brutus, for having killed Caesar" that Brutus not only had a right to kill Caesar because he was a tyrant but Brutus had a duty to do so and all law-abiding citizens should have done the same.
38. *Pennsylvania Journal*, 19 January 1774.
39. Joseph Galloway by profession was a lawyer but he was also the speaker of the house of assembly and afterwards a delegate to congress. Thomas Wharton was a merchant of the sect of Quakers. Both men had large property holdings and great influence in the colony. They supplied the capital for the *Pennsylvania Chronicle*. For more information see Thomas, *History of Printing in America*, 256–258.
40. For more on John Dickinson's life see Milton Flower, *John Dickinson: Conservative Revolutionary* (Charlottesville, VA: University Press of Virginia, 1983), 1–47.
41. Flower, *John Dickinson*, 1–47.
42. The entire collection can be seen in Forrest McDonald's *Empire and Nation: Letters from a Farmer in Pennsylvania* (Indianapolis: Liberty Fund, 1999).
43. Both were reprinted in Pennsylvania newspapers before. *Cato's Letters* Number 106 was reprinted in the *American Weekly Mercury* on 10 April 1729 and Number 10 was reprinted in the *Pennsylvania Journal* on 28 June 1764. Then the *Pennsylvania Gazette* reprinted Number 106 afterwards on 31 December 1767.
44. *Farmer's Letter*, Number II.
45. *Farmer's Letter*, Number V and *Cato's Letters*, Number 106.
46. *Farmer's Letter*, Number V and *Cato's Letters*, Number 106.
47. *Farmer's Letter*, Number VI and *Cato's Letters*, Number 38.
48. *Farmer's Letter*, Number IX and *Cato's Letters*, Number 125.
49. *Farmer's Letter*, Number XI and *Cato's Letters*, Numbers 70 and 125.

Conclusion

Trenchard and Gordon's works were reprinted in urban colonial newspapers when and where political elites attempted to entice a part of the populace into politics in order to gain its support. Before the 1760s, Trenchard and Gordon's essays appeared in colonies where politics were discussed in newspapers. Trenchard and Gordon's essays were usually used as opposition literature. Trenchard and Gordon helped shape opposition thought in urban areas such as New York City, Boston, and Philadelphia.

In Massachusetts and New York newspapers their works were reprinted during controversies that led to a battle in the press. Their works were used in newspapers that were created to oppose the establishment press.

This study also showed that Philadelphia newspapers were the most active in reprinting essays and the essays were reprinted in well-established newspapers early on. A split in authority between the proprietor and the Assembly complicated Pennsylvania politics. The existence of these two establishments encouraged the development of popular politics and the use of opposition literature. Since politics in Pennsylvania was a public concern, controversies were brought to the people in newspapers and warranted the reprinting of Trenchard and Gordon's essays.

The only southern newspaper that reprinted any of Trenchard and Gordon's essays before 1760 was the *South Carolina Gazette*. Because of the hierarchical politics of the colony, debates within the government institutions were frequent. The political culture that existed in New York, Pennsylvania, and Massachusetts, did not develop to the same extent in the south during the eighteenth century. South Carolinians preferred to engage in debates face to face. A few reprints of essays from *Cato's Letters* did appear, however, when the governor decided to adjourn the assembly during a heated debate. Since the governor would not allow discussion of the issues, one newspaper editor printed several of Trenchard and Gordon's essays in opposition, in effect, to the governor's actions. This was the only time Trenchard and Gordon's works were used before 1760 in the southern region.

This study showed that colonists living in Maryland, Rhode Island, North Carolina, Virginia, Georgia, and outside the urban centers of New York City, Philadelphia, and Boston may not have read Trenchard and Gordon's essays in newspapers. Trenchard and Gordon's works were not uniformly reprinted in the colonies before the 1760s.

Colonists used Trenchard and Gordon's works differently after 1760. A select number of essays from the *Cato's Letters* series were reprinted in newspapers throughout the colonies. Their works were no longer limited to newspapers in the urban areas. After 1760, Trenchard and Gordon's essays were also reprinted in newspapers in Virginia, Georgia, Maryland, Rhode Island, and Connecticut. The most widespread parts of *Cato's Letters* were reprinted as part of John Dickinson's series, *Letters From a Farmer in Pennsylvania*. More than 80% of the English newspapers in the North American colonies reprinted Dickinson's essays.[1] Dickinson's essays helped disseminate a few select ideas from Cato to a large percentage of the populace in the 1760s and 1770s.

Selections from Trenchard and Gordon's works appeared in opposition newspapers in Pennsylvania, New York, and Massachusetts after the 1760s as they did at highly politicized times earlier in the century. Their works, however, also appeared in establishment newspapers in these colonies. Moreover, Trenchard and Gordon's essays, as part of Dickinson's *Farmers Letters*, appeared in establishment newspapers in colonies that had not encouraged popular politics during the first half of the eighteenth century such as Virginia, South Carolina, and Georgia.

Trenchard and Gordon's significance should be recognized to the degree that their essays reinforced a political culture that encouraged the participation of lower and middling groups and rejected deferential society in Pennsylvania, New York, and Massachusetts before 1760. Then, their significance in other colonies after 1760 was that they encouraged popular politics in response to Parliament's policies regarding the colonies.

This study indicates the limited use of Trenchard and Gordon's works in colonial newspapers when considered overall. Of the 144 *Cato's Letters*, fewer than half were ever reprinted in colonial newspapers during the eighteenth century. Because only a limited number of Trenchard and Gordon's essays were reprinted, newspaper readers knew only a few of Trenchard and Gordon's ideas. On many occasions, the colonial printers used Trenchard and Gordon's essays in ways that were not intended by the authors because the essays were taken out of context. These are important issues to raise because one should no longer state that in general Trenchard and Gordon's works formed the *ideological* foundation of the American Revolution. Their works were important but only for how some people decided to use specific sections.

Trenchard and Gordon's works were significant because their works inculcated a different political culture in the colonies. Their works were used as opposition literature in newspapers. This encouraged middle and lower classes, traditionally outside the elite political structure, to become involved in politics. This eventually gave Americans the language needed to oppose British policies during the 1760s and 1770s. Colonists in Pennsylvania, New York, and Massachusetts rehearsed the role of the active citizen in their local areas during the first half of the century. In these areas, political elites were encouraging popular politics when it served the interest of a particular elite group. The unintentional result was that this gave colonists the vocabulary they eventually used to justify opposing British policies. The way their works were used taught colonists a mode of action, which laid the groundwork for the American Revolution.

NOTE

1. Out of the 23 English newspapers, 19 of them reprinted John Dickinson's *Farmer's Letters* series. See Carl F. Kaestle's article "The Public Reaction to John Dickinson's Farmer's Letters." *Proceedings of the American Antiquarian Society* Volume 78 (Worcester, MA: Society of American Antiquarian, 1969), 351.

Appendix One

Trenchard and Gordon's Works For Sale in Colonial Newspapers

Where	Newspaper	Cato's Letters	Independent Whig	Gordon's Tacitus
New York	New York Mercury	1753 July 16	1753 July 16	
New York	New York Mercury	1753 August 27	1753 August 27	
New York	New York Mercury	1753 September 3	1753 September 3	
New York	New York Gazette	1769 April 24		
Pennsylvania	American Weekly Mercury	1737 September 22	28 November 1745	
Pennsylvania	American Weekly Mercury		10 December 1745	
Pennsylvania	Pennsylvania Gazette	1742 December 14	1739 January 18	1745 March 5
Pennsylvania	Pennsylvania Gazette	1743 May 19	1739 March 22	1758 March 2
Pennsylvania	Pennsylvania Gazette	1748 January 26	1740 February 7	1759 February 22
Pennsylvania	Pennsylvania Gazette	1749 March 14	1740 September 25	1762 May 27
Pennsylvania	Pennsylvania Gazette	1749 June 22	1742 December 14	1776 January 24
Pennsylvania	Pennsylvania Gazette	1749 October 12	1743 May 19	1777 May 28
Pennsylvania	Pennsylvania Gazette	1749 December 19	1747 February 3	1744 November 11
Pennsylvania	Pennsylvania Gazette	1750 February 6	1747 February 10	1750 February 5
Pennsylvania	Pennsylvania Gazette	1758 March 2	1747 April 9	1751 March 28
Pennsylvania	Pennsylvania Gazette	1776 January 24	1749 October 12	1754 December 12
Pennsylvania	Pennsylvania Gazette		1749 December 19	1756 January 29
Pennsylvania	Pennsylvania Gazette		1750 February 6	1756 May 6
Pennsylvania	Pennsylvania Gazette		1751 December 10	1756 May 13
Pennsylvania	Pennsylvania Gazette		1753 November 1	1756 May 27
Pennsylvania	Pennsylvania Gazette		1754 July 18	1756 June 3
Pennsylvania	Pennsylvania Gazette		1758 March 2	1759 June 7
Pennsylvania	Pennsylvania Gazette		1759 June 21	1762 June 10
Pennsylvania	Pennsylvania Gazette		1761 October 29	1762 December 2
Pennsylvania	Pennsylvania Gazette		1766 August 7	1763 November 10

Colony	Newspaper	Date	Date
Pennsylvania	Pennsylvania Gazette		1767 January 15
Pennsylvania	Pennsylvania Gazette		1776 January 24
Pennsylvania	Pennsylvania Journal	1743 November 3	1751 March 28
Pennsylvania	Pennsylvania Journal	1743 November 10	1756 May 6
Pennsylvania	Pennsylvania Journal	1744 November 11	1756 May 13
Pennsylvania	Pennsylvania Journal	1749 October 26	1756 May 27
Pennsylvania	Pennsylvania Journal	1751 March 28	1759 June 7
Pennsylvania	Pennsylvania Journal	1754 December 12	1760 July 17
Pennsylvania	Pennsylvania Journal	1755 May 22	1760 July 24
Pennsylvania	Pennsylvania Journal	1755 August 7	1760 September 11
Pennsylvania	Pennsylvania Journal	1755 September 4	
Pennsylvania	Pennsylvania Journal	1759 June 7	
Pennsylvania	Pennsylvania Journal	1769 November 30	
Pennsylvania	Pennsylvania Journal	1769 December 14	
Pennsylvania	Pennsylvania Chronicle	1768 September 5	
Massachusetts	Boston News Letter	1761 June 11	1761 July 23
Massachusetts	Boston News Letter	1761 June 18	1761 July 30
Massachusetts	Boston News Letter	1761 July 16	1762 February 18
Massachusetts	Boston News Letter	1761 July 23	1762 February 25
Massachusetts	Boston News Letter	1761 July 30	1762 March 2
Massachusetts	Boston News Letter	1762 February 18	1762 March 11
Massachusetts	Independent Advertiser (Boston)	1748 July 25	1748 July 25
Massachusetts	Independent Advertiser (Boston)	1748 August 1	1748 August 1
Massachusetts	Boston Gazette	1761 December 7	1748 December 7
Massachusetts	Boston Gazette	1761 December 14	1748 December 14
Rhode Island	Newport Mercury	1764 August 6	

Appendix Two

Cato's Letters When and Where Reprinted in the North American British Colonies during the Eighteenth Century

Cato's Letters	Subject	Where Reprinted	When Reprinted
10	Taxes	Pennsylvania Journal	1764 June 28
15	Speech Freedom	New England Courant	1722 July 2
15	Speech Freedom	New York Weekly Journal (NYWJ)	1733 February 18
15	Speech Freedom	American Weekly Mercury (AWM)	1733 March 5
15	Speech Freedom	New York Weekly Journal (NYWJ)	1734 November 11
15	Speech Freedom	South Carolina Gazette	1736 June 5
15	Speech Freedom	Pennsylvania Gazette	1737 November 10
15	Speech Freedom	Boston Evening Post	1742 April 12
15	Speech Freedom	South Carolina Gazette	1748 July 9
15	Speech Freedom	Independent Reflector (New York)	1753 August 30
15	Speech Freedom	Boston Gazette and Country Journal	1755 April 21
15	Speech Freedom	Pennsylvania Journal	1758 February 23
15	Speech Freedom	New York Journal or General Advertiser	1767 March 19
15	Speech Freedom	New York Journal or General Advertiser	1767 November 19
15	Speech Freedom	Boston Gazette and Country Journal	1767 November 9
15	Speech Freedom	Massachusetts Spy	1771 March 28
15	Speech Freedom	Massachusetts Spy	1771 March 7
17	Wicked ministers	Pennsylvania Journal	1758 March 9
18	Public corruption	New York Journal or General Advertiser	1767 April 9
23	Letter from Brutus	Massachusetts Spy	1773 May 13
24	Government	Boston Gazette and Country Journal	1755 June 23
26	Corruption	New York Journal or General Advertiser	1767 April 9
27	Corruption	American Weekly Mercury (AWM)	1738 April 13
27	Corruption	New York Mercury	1757 March 21
31	Human Nature	Independent Reflector (New York)	1753 January 25
32	Reflection on Libeling	New England Courant	1721 September 4
32	Reflection on Libeling	New York Weekly Journal (NYWJ)	1733 February 23
32	Reflection on Libeling	New York Gazette or Weekly Post-Boy	1770 April 2
33	Natural Encroach of power	New England Courant	1721 October 16

Page	Topic	Publication	Date
33	Natural Encroach of power	New England Courant	1721 October 23
33	Natural Encroach of power	American Weekly Mercury (AWM)	1722 June 14
33	Natural Encroach of power	New York Weekly Journal (NYWJ)	1733 March 11
33	Natural Encroach of power	New York Journal or General Advertiser	1774 October 20
34	Flattery	New England Courant	1721 October 2
34	Flattery	New England Courant	1721 October 9
34	Flattery	American Weekly Mercury (AWM)	1722 March 22
34	Flattery	Massachusetts Spy	1771 July 18
35	Public Spirit	American Weekly Mercury (AWM)	1722 April 12
35	Public Spirit	Pennsylvania Gazette	1734 August 12
35	Public Spirit	American Weekly Mercury (AWM)	1738 April 13
35	Public Spirit	Independent Advertiser (Boston)	1748 January 25
36	Loyalty	American Weekly Mercury (AWM)	1722 May 31
37	Good/Evil Magistrates	New York Weekly Journal (NYWJ)	1735 July 21
37	Good/Evil Magistrates	South Carolina Gazette	1748 July 25
37	Good/Evil Magistrates	Independent Advertiser (Boston)	1748 May 1748
38	Judge government officials	American Weekly Mercury (AWM)	1722 February 13
38	Judge government officials	New York Weekly Journal (NYWJ)	1733 December 10
38	Judge government officials	American Weekly Mercury (AWM)	1733 September 20
38	Judge government officials	New York Weekly Journal (NYWJ)	1735 July 21
38	Judge government officials	Pennsylvania Gazette	1737 December 1
38	Judge government officials	Pennsylvania Gazette	1737 November 10
38	Judge government officials	American Weekly Mercury (AWM)	1738 April 27
38	Judge government officials	Pennsylvania Gazette	1738 May 11
38	Judge government officials	South Carolina Gazette	1748 August 1
38	Judge government officials	Independent Advertiser (Boston)	1748 February 29
38	Judge government officials	Independent Reflector (New York)	1752 December 21
38	Judge government officials	Boston Gazette and Country Journal	1755 May 12
38	Judge government officials	Boston Gazette and Country Journal	1755 May 19

(continued)

Cato's Letters	Subject	Where Reprinted	When Reprinted
38	Judge government officials	Pennsylvania Journal	1770 March 15 (Zenger)
38	Judge government officials	New York Journal or General Advertiser	1770 March 29 (Zenger)
38	Judge government officials	Pennsylvania Journal	1773 March 26
38	Judge government officials	Pennsylvania Evening Post	1775 March 28
38	Judge government officials	Pennsylvania Evening Post	1775 March 30
38	Passions	American Weekly Mercury (AWM)	1729 September 11
39	Selfish spirit of man	American Weekly Mercury (AWM)	1722 March 10
40	Natural Encroach of power	New York Weekly Journal (NYWJ)	1735 July 14 (cont.)
42	Nature of laws	New York Weekly Journal (NYWJ)	1735 July 7
42	Equality/inequality of men	American Weekly Mercury (AWM)	1730 April 2
45	Equality/inequality of men	Independent Reflector (New York)	1753 August 2
45	Vindication of Brutus	New York Weekly Journal (NYWJ)	1739 April 2 (cont.)
56	Vindication of Brutus	New York Weekly Journal (NYWJ)	1739 April 9 (cont.)
56	Vindication of Brutus	New York Weekly Journal (NYWJ)	1739 March 26
56	Liberty—unalienable right	Pennsylvania Gazette	1736 April 8
59	Government	New York Weekly Journal (NYWJ)	1735 August 25
60	Government	New York Weekly Journal (NYWJ)	1735 September 1
60	Government	Independent Reflector (New York)	1753 February 22
60	Government	New York Journal or General Advertiser	1766 December 11
60	Government	Massachusetts Spy	1771 April 4
61	Free Government	American Weekly Mercury (AWM)	1738 April 27
62	Liberty vs. Slavery	New York Weekly Journal (NYWJ)	1735 September 15 (cont.)
62	Liberty vs. Slavery	New York Weekly Journal (NYWJ)	1735 September 23 (cont.)
62	Liberty vs. Slavery	New York Weekly Journal (NYWJ)	1735 September 9
62	Liberty vs. Slavery	American Weekly Mercury (AWM)	1738 April 13
62	Liberty vs. Slavery	New York Journal or General Advertiser	1766 December 11
65	Military virtue	New York Journal or General Advertiser	1766 December 24
67	Effects of Civil Liberty	Independent Advertiser (Boston)	1749 June 26
69	Choice of representatives	American Weekly Mercury (AWM)	1729 September 11

Page	Topic	Newspaper	Date
70	Choice of representatives	American Weekly Mercury (AWM)	1729 September 18
70	Choice of representatives	New Hampshire Gazette (Portsmouth)	1765 August 30
75	Restraint needed for rulers	New York Weekly Journal (NYWJ)	1734 May 27
80	Parties in England	Independent Reflector (New York)	1753 February 22
94	Standing armies	New York Journal or General Advertiser	1774 October 6
95	Standing armies	New York Journal or General Advertiser	1774 October 6
96	Parties in England	Independent Reflector (New York)	1753 February 22
96	Parties in England	Pennsylvania Evening Post	1775 April 4
96	Parties in England	Pennsylvania Evening Post	1775 April 6 (cont.)
97	Governors	Pennsylvania Journal	1769 August 17
99	Important duty of Parliament	South Carolina Gazette	1749 March 13
100	Libels	American Weekly Mercury (AWM)	1728 March 13
100	Libels	New York Weekly Journal (NYWJ)	1734 December 9
100	Libels	Boston Evening Post	1742 May 17
100	Libels	Massachusetts Spy	1771 April 19
101	Second Discourse on libels	Massachusetts Spy	1771 April 25
102	Virtue	American Weekly Mercury (AWM)	1729 April 10
106	colonies	American Weekly Mercury (AWM)	1729 April 24
106	colonies	Pennsylvania Gazette	1767 December 31
108	Virtues	Independent Reflector (New York)	1753 December 21
111	Liberty	American Weekly Mercury (AWM)	1730 April 23
111	Liberty	American Weekly Mercury (AWM)	1730 April 9
112	Liberty	New York Weekly Journal (NYWJ)	1733 January 28
113	Cato's adversaries	Massachusetts Spy	1771 December 19
115	Nature of power	New York Weekly Journal (NYWJ)	1734 May 27
115	Nature of power	Independent Reflector (New York)	1753 January 25
115	Nature of power	Pennsylvania Journal	1768 May 5
123	Religious Enthusiasm	American Weekly Mercury (AWM)	1730 May 7
124	Enthusiasm	American Weekly Mercury (AWM)	1730 May 21

(continued)

Cato's Letters	Subject	Where Reprinted	When Reprinted
124	Enthusiasm	American Weekly Mercury (AWM)	1730 May 28 (cont.)
128	Clergy	American Weekly Mercury (AWM)	1724 February 4 (cont.)
128	Clergy	Boston News Letter	1724 March 5
128	Clergy	Pennsylvania Gazette	1736 June 3
130	Clergy	American Weekly Mercury (AWM)	1724 February 18 (cont.)
130	Clergy	American Weekly Mercury (AWM)	1724 February 4 (cont.)
131	Reverence	American Weekly Mercury (AWM)	1722 May 31
131	Reverence	American Weekly Mercury (AWM)	1723 December 31
131	Reverence	American Weekly Mercury (AWM)	1733 December 31
131	Reverence	New York Weekly Journal (NYWJ)	1753 July 19
131	Reverence	Independent Reflector (New York)	1753 September 20
Preface	Preface	Independent Reflector (New York)	1752 November 30

Appendix Three

Newspapers where essays from *Cato's Letters* appeared from 1721–1776

#	Subject	Where Reprinted	When Reprinted	Colony
32	Speech Freedom	*New England Courant*	1721 September 4	Massachusetts
34	Flattery	*New England Courant*	1721 October 2	Massachusetts
34	Flattery	*New England Courant*	1721 October 9 (cont.)	Massachusetts
33	Human Nature	*New England Courant*	1721 October 16	Massachusetts
33	Human Nature	*New England Courant*	1721 October 23 (cont.)	Massachusetts
57	Honor	*New England Courant*	1722 April 2 (summary)	Massachusetts
27	Corruption	*New England Courant*	1722 April 30	Massachusetts
15	Speech Freedom	*New England Courant*	1722 July 2	Massachusetts
31	Human Nature	*New England Courant*	1722 July 16	Massachusetts
128	Clergy	*Boston News Letter*	1724 March 5	Massachusetts
15	Speech Freedom	*Boston Evening Post*	1742 April 12	Massachusetts
100	Speech Freedom	*Boston Evening Post*	1742 May 17	Massachusetts
45	Human Nature	*Independent Advertiser*	1748 January 11	Massachusetts
35	Public Spirit	*Independent Advertiser*	1748 January 25	Massachusetts
38	Judge government officials	*Independent Advertiser*	1748 February 29	Massachusetts
37	Human Nature	*Independent Advertiser*	1748 May 16	Massachusetts
26	Corruption	*Independent Advertiser*	1748 June 13	Massachusetts
67	Liberty	*Independent Advertiser*	1748 June 26	Massachusetts
43	Human Nature	*Independent Advertiser*	1748 August 22	Massachusetts
73	Liberty	*Independent Advertiser*	1748 December 31	Massachusetts
15	Speech Freedom	*Boston Gazette and Country Journal*	1755 April 21	Massachusetts
38	Judge government officials	*Boston Gazette and Country Journal*	1755 May 12	Massachusetts
38	Judge government officials	*Boston Gazette and Country Journal*	1755 May 19 (cont.)	Massachusetts
24	Government	*Boston Gazette and Country Journal*	1755 June 23	Massachusetts
15	Speech Freedom	*Boston Gazette and Country Journal*	1756 April 26	Massachusetts
15	Speech Freedom	*Boston Gazette and Country Journal*	1767 November 9	Massachusetts
70	Judge government officials	*Boston Gazette and Country Journal*	1767 November 9	Massachusetts
15	Speech Freedom	*Massachusetts Spy*	1771 March 7	Massachusetts
15	Speech Freedom	*Massachusetts Spy*	1771 March 28	Massachusetts

60	Government	Massachusetts Spy	1771 April 4	Massachusetts
100	Speech Freedom	Massachusetts Spy	1771 April 19	Massachusetts
101	Speech Freedom	Massachusetts Spy	1771 April 25	Massachusetts
15	Speech Freedom	Massachusetts Spy	1771 May 6	Massachusetts
34	Flattery	Massachusetts Spy	1771 July 18	Massachusetts
112	Human Nature	Massachusetts Spy	1771 December 19	Massachusetts
113	Concerning Cato's Adversaries	Massachusetts Spy	1771 December 26	Massachusetts
23	Letter from Brutus	Massachusetts Spy	1773 May 13	Massachusetts
73	Liberty	New Hampshire Gazette (Portsmouth)	1765 August 30	New Hampshire
38	Judge government officials	New York Weekly Journal	1733 December 10	New York
131	Reverence	New York Weekly Journal	1733 December 31	New York
112	Liberty	New York Weekly Journal	1734 January 28	New York
14	Corruption	New York Weekly Journal	1734 February 11	New York
15	Speech Freedom	New York Weekly Journal	1734 February 18	New York
32	Reflection on Libeling	New York Weekly Journal	1734 February 25	New York
32	Reflection on Libeling	New York Weekly Journal	1734 March 4 (cont.)	New York
33	Human Nature	New York Weekly Journal	1734 March 11	New York
75	Human Nature	New York Weekly Journal	1734 May 27	New York
115	Human Nature	New York Weekly Journal	1734 May 27	New York
15	Speech Freedom	New York Weekly Journal	1734 November 11	New York
42	Human Nature	New York Weekly Journal	1735 July 7	New York
42	Human Nature	New York Weekly Journal	1735 July 14	New York
37	Human Nature	New York Weekly Journal	1735 July 21	New York
60	Government	New York Weekly Journal	1735 August 25	New York
60	Government	New York Weekly Journal	1735 September 1 (cont.)	New York
62	Liberty	New York Weekly Journal	1735 September 8	New York
62	Liberty	New York Weekly Journal	1735 September 15 (cont.)	New York
62	Liberty	New York Weekly Journal	1735 September 23 (cont.)	New York
56	Vindication of Brutus	New York Weekly Journal	1739 March 26	New York

(continued)

#	Subject	Where Reprinted	When Reprinted	Colony
56	Vindication of Brutus	New York Weekly Journal	1739 April 2 (cont.)	New York
56	Vindication of Brutus	New York Weekly Journal	1739 April 9 (cont.)	New York
0	Preface	Independent Reflector	1752 November 30	New York
38	Judge government officials	Independent Reflector	1752 December 21	New York
31	Human Nature	Independent Reflector	1753 January 25	New York
115	Human Nature	Independent Reflector	1753 January 25	New York
60	Government	Independent Reflector	1753 February 22	New York
80	Factions	Independent Reflector	1753 February 22	New York
96	Factions	Independent Reflector	1753 February 22	New York
131	Reverence	Independent Reflector	1753 July 19	New York
45	Human Nature	Independent Reflector	1753 August 2	New York
31	Human Nature	Independent Reflector	1753 August 23	New York
131	Reverence	Independent Reflector	1753 September 20	New York
108	Virtue	Independent Reflector	1753 December 21	New York
27	Corruption	New York Mercury	1757 March 21	New York
60	Government	New York Journal	1766 December 11	New York
62	Liberty	New York Journal	1766 December 11	New York
65	Virtue	New York Journal	1766 December 24	New York
15	Speech Freedom	New York Journal	1767 March 19	New York
18	Corruption	New York Journal	1767 April 9	New York
26	Corruption	New York Journal	1767 April 9	New York
15	Speech Freedom	New York Journal	1767 November 19	New York
38	Judge government officials	New York Journal	1770 March 29 (Zenger)	New York
94	Standing Armies	New York Journal	1774 October 6	New York
95	Standing Armies	New York Journal	1774 October 6	New York
33	Human Nature	New York Journal	1774 October 20	New York
32	Speech Freedom	New York Gazette or Weekly Post-Boy	1770 April 2	New York
38	Judge government officials	American Weekly Mercury (AWM)	1722 February 13	Pennsylvania
40	Human Nature	American Weekly Mercury (AWM)	1722 March 10	Pennsylvania

34	Flattery	American Weekly Mercury (AWM)	1722 March 22	Pennsylvania
35	Public Spirit	American Weekly Mercury (AWM)	1722 April 12	Pennsylvania
36	Loyalty	American Weekly Mercury (AWM)	1722 May 31	Pennsylvania
33	Natural Encroach of power	American Weekly Mercury (AWM)	1722 June 14	Pennsylvania
134	Human Nature	American Weekly Mercury (AWM)	1723 December 24	Pennsylvania
131	Reverence	American Weekly Mercury (AWM)	1723 December 31	Pennsylvania
131	Reverence	American Weekly Mercury (AWM)	1724 January 7 (cont.)	Pennsylvania
128	Clergy	American Weekly Mercury (AWM)	1724 February 4	Pennsylvania
128	Clergy	American Weekly Mercury (AWM)	1724 February 11 (cont.)	Pennsylvania
130	Clergy	American Weekly Mercury (AWM)	1724 February 18	Pennsylvania
130	Clergy	American Weekly Mercury (AWM)	1724 February 25	Pennsylvania
100	Speech Freedom	American Weekly Mercury (AWM)	1729 March 13	Pennsylvania
102	Virtue	American Weekly Mercury (AWM)	1729 April 10	Pennsylvania
106	Colonies	American Weekly Mercury (AWM)	1729 April 24	Pennsylvania
39	Human Nature	American Weekly Mercury (AWM)	1729 September 11	Pennsylvania
40	Human Nature	American Weekly Mercury (AWM)	1729 September 11	Pennsylvania
45	Human Nature	American Weekly Mercury (AWM)	1730 April 2	Pennsylvania
111	Liberty	American Weekly Mercury (AWM)	1730 April 9	Pennsylvania
111	Liberty	American Weekly Mercury (AWM)	1730 April 23 (cont.)	Pennsylvania
123	Religious Enthusiasm	American Weekly Mercury (AWM)	1730 May 7	Pennsylvania
123	Enthusiasm	American Weekly Mercury (AWM)	1730 May 14 (cont.)	Pennsylvania
124	Enthusiasm	American Weekly Mercury (AWM)	1730 May 21	Pennsylvania
124	Enthusiasm	American Weekly Mercury (AWM)	1730 May 28 (cont.)	Pennsylvania
59	Liberty	American Weekly Mercury (AWM)	1732 March 30	Pennsylvania
15	Speech Freedom	American Weekly Mercury (AWM)	1734 March 5	Pennsylvania
38	Judge government officials	American Weekly Mercury (AWM)	1734 September 20	Pennsylvania
27	Corruption	American Weekly Mercury (AWM)	1738 April 13	Pennsylvania
35	Public Spirit	American Weekly Mercury (AWM)	1738 April 13	Pennsylvania
62	Liberty	American Weekly Mercury (AWM)	1738 April 13	Pennsylvania

(continued)

#	Subject	Where Reprinted	When Reprinted	Colony
38	Judge government officials	American Weekly Mercury (AWM)	1738 April 27	Pennsylvania
61	Free Government	American Weekly Mercury (AWM)	1738 April 27	Pennsylvania
27	Liberty	American Weekly Mercury (AWM)	1738 May 18	Pennsylvania
35	Public Spirit	Pennsylvania Gazette	1734 August 15	Pennsylvania
59	Liberty	Pennsylvania Gazette	1736 April 8	Pennsylvania
128	Clergy	Pennsylvania Gazette	1736 June 3	Pennsylvania
15	Speech Freedom	Pennsylvania Gazette	1737 November 10	Pennsylvania
38	Judge government officials	Pennsylvania Gazette	1737 November 10	Pennsylvania
38	Judge government officials	Pennsylvania Gazette	1737 December 1	Pennsylvania
38	Judge government officials	Pennsylvania Gazette	1738 May 11	Pennsylvania
106	Colonies	Pennsylvania Gazette	1767 December 31	Pennsylvania
15	Speech Freedom	Pennsylvania Journal	1758 February 23	Pennsylvania
17	Human Nature	Pennsylvania Journal	1758 March 9	Pennsylvania
10	Taxes	Pennsylvania Journal	1764 June 28	Pennsylvania
115	Human Nature	Pennsylvania Journal	1768 May 5	Pennsylvania
97	Governors	Pennsylvania Journal	1769 August 17	Pennsylvania
38	Judge government officials	Pennsylvania Journal	1770 March 15 (Zenger)	Pennsylvania
38	Judge government officials	Pennsylvania Journal	1773 May 26	Pennsylvania
38	Judge government officials	Pennsylvania Journal	1775 March 28	Pennsylvania
38	Judge government officials	Pennsylvania Journal	1775 March 30 (cont.)	Pennsylvania
96	Factions	Pennsylvania Journal	1775 April 4	Pennsylvania
96	Factions	Pennsylvania Journal	1775 April 6 (cont.)	Pennsylvania
15	Speech Freedom	South Carolina Gazette	1736 June 5	South Carolina
15	Speech Freedom	South Carolina Gazette	1748 July 9	South Carolina
37	Human Nature	South Carolina Gazette	1748 July 23	South Carolina
38	Judge government officials	South Carolina Gazette	1748 August 1	South Carolina
99	Important duty of Parliament	South Carolina Gazette	1749 March 13	South Carolina

Bibliography

PRIMARY SOURCES: NEWSPAPERS

Boston Newspapers

Boston Chronicle
Boston Evening Post
Boston Gazette
Boston Gazette and Country Journal
Boston News Letter
Boston Weekly Newsletter
The Censor
Independent Advertiser
Massachusetts Gazette
Massachusetts Spy
New England Courant
New England Weekly Journal
Weekly Rehearsal

Charleston Newspapers

South Carolina Gazette

New York Newspapers

Independent Reflector
New York Evening Post
New York Gazette (William Bradford)

New York Gazette (Weyman's)
New York Gazette and the Weekly Mercury
New York Gazette or Weekly Post-Boy
New York Journal or General Advertiser
New York Mercury
New York Weekly Journal

Philadelphia Newspapers

American Weekly Mercury
The Freeman's Journal or North American Intelligencer
Pennsylvania Chronicle and Universal Advertiser
Pennsylvania Evening Herald and the American Monitor
Pennsylvania Gazette
Pennsylvania Journal and Weekly Advertiser

Portsmouth, New Hampshire Newspapers

New Hampshire Gazette

Newport, Rhode Island Newspapers

Newport Mercury

PUBLISHED SECONDARY SOURCES: BOOKS

Anderson, Benedict. *Imagined Communities: Reflections on the Origin and Spread of Nationalism*. New York: Verso, 1983, 1991.

Appleby, Joyce. *Liberalism and Republicanism in the Historical Imagination*. Cambridge, MA: Harvard University Press, 1992.

Bailyn, Bernard. *The Origins of American Politics*. New York: Vintage Books, 1967.

──. *Ideological Origins of the American Revolution*. Cambridge, MA: Belknap Press, 1967; reprint, 1992.

──. *Pamphlets of the American Revolution 1750–1776*. Cambridge, MA: The Belknap Press of Harvard University Press, 1965.

──. and John B. Hench eds. *The Press and the American Revolution*. Worcester, MA: American Antiquarian Society, 1980.

Banning, Lance. *The Jeffersonian Persuasion: Evolution of a Party Ideology*. Ithaca, NY: Cornell University, 1978.

Bennett, G. V. *The Tory Crisis in Church and State 1688–1730: The career of Francis Atterbury Bishop of Rochester*. Oxford: Clarendon Press, 1975.

Black, Jeremy. *The English Press in the Eighteenth Century*. Philadelphia, PA: University of Pennsylvania Press, 1987.
Bond, Donovan H. and W. Reynolds McLeod eds. *Newsletters to Newspapers: Eighteenth-Century Journalism*. Morgantown, WV: The School of Journalism, West Virginia University, 1977.
Bonomi, Patricia U. *A Factious People: Politics and Society in Colonial New York*. New York: Columbia University Press, 1971.
———. *Under the Cope of Heaven: Religion, Society, and Politics in Colonial America*. New York: Oxford University Press, 1986.
Breen, T. H. *The Character of the Good Ruler: A Study of Puritan Political Ideas in New England, 1630–1730*. New Haven, CT: Yale University Press, 1970.
Brewer, John. *Party Ideology and Popular Politics at the accession of George III*. Cambridge, UK: University of Cambridge, 1976.
Brigham, Clarence S. *Journals and Journeymen: A Contribution to the History of Early American Newspapers*. Philadelphia, PA: University of Pennsylvania Press, 1950.
Brown, Richard D. *Knowledge Is Power: The Diffusion of Information in Early America, 1700–1865*. New York: Oxford University Press, 1989.
Bushman, Richard L. *King and People in Provincial Massachusetts*. Chapel Hill, NC: The University of North Carolina Press, 1985.
Carswell, John. *The South Sea Bubble*. London: Alan Sutton Publishing Ltd., 1960.
Clair, Colin. *A History of Printing in Britain*. New York: Oxford University Press, 1966.
Clark, Charles E. *The Public Prints: The Newspaper in Anglo-American Culture, 1665–1740*. New York: Oxford University Press, 1994.
Clark, J. C. D. *The Language of Liberty 1660–1832: Political discourse and social dynamics in the Anglo-American World*. Cambridge: Cambridge University Press, 1994.
Colbourn, Trevor. *The Lamp of Experience: Whig History and the Intellectual Origins of the American Revolution*. Chapel Hill: University of North Carolina Press, 1965; reprint, Indianapolis: Liberty Fund, 1998.
Colley, Linda. *In Defiance of Oligarchy: The Tory Party, 1714–1760*. New York: Cambridge University Press, 1982.
Cook, Elizabeth Christine. *Literary Influences in Colonial Newspapers: 1704–1750*. New York: Columbia University Press, 1912.
Copeland, David A. *Colonial American Newspapers: Character and Content*. Newark, NJ: University of Delaware Press, 1997.
Cottret, Bernard. *Bolingbroke's Political Writings: A Conservative Enlightenment*. New York: St. Martin's Press, Inc., 1997.
Cowles, Virginia. *The Great Swindle: The Story of the South Sea Bubble*. New York: Harper & Brothers Publishers, 1960.
Darnton, Robert. *The Forbidden Best-Sellers of Pre-Revolutionary France*. New York: W. W. Norton & Company, 1995.
Davidson, Cathy N. ed. *Reading in America: Literature & Social History*. Baltimore, MD: The Johns Hopkins University Press, 1989.

Davis, Richard Beale. *A Colonial Southern Bookshelf: Reading in the Eighteenth Century*. Athens, GA: The University of Georgia Press, 1979.

DeArmond, Anna Janney. *Andrew Bradford: Colonial Journalist*. New York: Greenwood Press, 1969.

Eisenstein, Elizabeth. *Print Culture and Enlightenment Thought*. Chapel Hill, NC: The University of North Carolina at Chapel Hill, 1986.

Flower, Milton E. *John Dickinson: Conservative Revolutionary*. Charlottesville, VA: University Press of Virginia, 1983.

Foord, Archibald S. *His Majesty's Opposition 1714–1830*. Oxford: At the Clarendon Press, 1964.

Gay, Peter. *The Enlightenment: An Interpretation*. New York: W. W. Norton & Company, 1969.

Gerrard, Christine. *The Patriot Opposition to Walpole: Politics, Poetry, and National Myth, 1725–1742*. Oxford: Clarendon Press, 1994.

Gilmore, William J. *Reading Becomes a Necessity of Life: Material and Cultural Life in Rural New England, 1780–1835*. Knoxville, TN: The University of Tennessee Press, 1989.

Greene, Evarts B. and Virginia D. Harrington. *American Population Before the Federal Census of 1790*. New York: Columbia University Press, 1932.

Greene, Jack P. *Peripheries and Center: Constitutional Development in the Extended Polities of the British Empire and the United States, 1607–1788*. Athens: The University of Georgia Press, 1986.

Gummere, Richard M. *The American Colonial Mind and the Classical Tradition: Essays in Comparative Culture*. Cambridge, MA: Harvard University Press, 1963.

Habermas, Jurgen. *The Structural Transformation of the Public Sphere: An Inquiry into a Category of Bourgeois Society*. Cambridge, MA: The MIT Press, 1991, 1996.

Hall, David D. *Worlds of Wonder, Days of Judgment: Popular Religious Belief in Early New England*. Cambridge, MA: Harvard University Press, 1989.

———. *Cultures of Print: Essays in the History of the Book*. Amherst, MA: University of Massachusetts Press, 1996.

Hamowy, Ronald. Ed. *Cato's Letters: or, Essays on Liberty, Civil and Religious, And other Important Subjects*. Indianapolis, IN: Liberty Fund, 1995.

Harris, Robert. *A Patriot Press: National Politics and the London Press in the 1740s*. Oxford: Clarendon Press, 1993.

Hutson, James H. *Pennsylvania Politics 1746–1770: The Movement for Royal Government and Its Consequences*. Princeton, NJ: Princeton University Press, 1972.

Jacobson, David L. *John Dickinson and The Revolution in Pennsylvania, 1764–1776*. Los Angeles, CA: University of California Press, 1965.

Joyce, William L. and David Hall, eds., *Printing and Society in Early America*. Worchester, MA: American Antiquarian Society, 1983.

Judd, Jacob. *Aspects of Early New York Society and Politics*. Tarrytown, NY: Sleepy Hollow Restorations, 1974.

Klein, Milton. *The Independent Reflector, or Weekly Essays on Sundry Important Subjects more Particularly Adapted to the Province of New York*. Cambridge, MA: The Belknap Press of Harvard University Press, 1963.

Kobre, Sidney. *The Development of the Colonial Newspaper*. Gloucester, MA: Peter Smith, 1960.
Kramnick, Isaac. *Bolingbroke and His Circle: The Politics of Nostalgia in the Age of Walpole*. Cambridge, MA: Harvard University Press, 1968.
———. *Republicanism and Bourgeois Radicalism: Political Ideology in Late Eighteenth-Century England and America*. Ithaca and London: Cornell University Press, 1990.
Labaree, Benjamin W. *Colonial Massachusetts: A History*. Millwood, NY: KTO Press, 1979.
Land, Aubrey C. *The Dulanys of Maryland: A Biographical Study of Daniel Dulany, The elder and Daniel Dulany, The Younger*. Baltimore, MD: The Johns Hopkins Press, 1955.
Landsman, Ned C. *From Colonials to Provincials: American Thought and Culture 1680–1760*. New York: Twayne Publishers, 1997.
Laprade, W. T. *Public Opinion and Politics in Eighteenth Century England To the Fall of Walpole*. New York: The Macmillan Company, 1936.
Levy, Leonard. *Legacy of Suppression: Freedom of Speech and Press in Early American History*. Cambridge, MA: The Belknap Press of Harvard University Press, 1964.
———. *Emergence of a Free Press*. New York: Oxford University Press, 1985.
Lockridge, Kenneth A. *Literacy in Colonial New England: An Enquiry into the Social Context of Literacy in the Early Modern West*. New York: W. W. Norton, 1974.
Maier, Pauline. *From Resistance to Revolution: Colonial radicals and the development of American opposition to Britain, 1765–1776*. New York: Alfred. A. Knopf, 1972; reprint, New York: W. W. Norton & Company, 1991.
May, Henry F. *The Enlightenment in America*. Oxford: Oxford University Press, 1976.
McDonald, Forrest. *Novus Ordo Seclorum: The Intellectual Origins of the Constitution*. Lawrence, KS: University of Kansas, 1985.
McMahon, Marie P. *The Radical Whigs, John Trenchard and Thomas Gordon: Libertarian Loyalists to the New House of Hanover*. Lanham, MD: University Press of America, 1990.
Morgan, Edmund S. *Inventing the People: The Rise of Popular Sovereignty in England and America*. New York: W. W. Norton & Company, 1989.
Mott, Frank Luther. *The News in America*. Cambridge, MA: Harvard University Press, 1962.
Nash, Gary B. *The Urban Crucible: Social Change, Political Consciousness, and the Origins of the American Revolution*. Cambridge, MA: Harvard University Press, 1979.
Pencak, William. *War, Politics, & Revolution in Provincial Massachusetts*. Boston, MA: Northeastern University Press, 1981.
Pettit, Alexander. *Illusory Consensus: Bolingbroke and the Polemical Response to Walpole, 1730–1737*. Newark, NJ: University of Delaware Press, 1997.
Pocock, J. G. A. *The Machiavellian Moment: Florentine Political thought and the Atlantic Republican Tradition*. Princeton, NJ: Princeton University Press, 1975.
Robbins, Caroline. *The Eighteenth-Century Commonwealthman: Studies in the Transmission, Development and Circumstance of English Liberal Thought from the Restoration of Charles II until the War with the Thirteen Colonies*. Cambridge, MA: Harvard University Press, 1961.

Rossiter, Clinton. *Seedtime of the Republic: The Origin of the American Tradition of Political Liberty*. New York: Harcourt, Brace and Company, 1953.
Schlesinger, Arthur M. *Prelude to Independence: The Newspaper War on Britain, 1764–1776*. New York: Alfred A. Knopf, 1958.
Schutz, John A. *William Shirley: King's Governor of Massachusetts*. Chapel Hill, NC: University of North Carolina Press, 1961.
Shepherd, William Robert. *History of Proprietary Government in Pennsylvania*. New York: AMS Press, Inc., 1967.
Silver, Rollo G. *The American Printer 1787–1825*. Charlottesville, VA: The University Press of Virginia, 1967.
Sirmans, M. Eugene. *Colonial South Carolina: A Political History 1663–1763*. Chapel Hill, NC: University of North Carolina Press, 1966.
Sloan, William David and Julie Hedgepeth Williams. *The Early American Press, 1690–1783*. Westport, CT: Greenwood Press, 1994.
Sutherland, Stella H. *Population Distribution in Colonial America*. New York: AMS Press, Inc. 1966.
Thomas, Isaiah. *The History of Printing in America: With a Biography of Printers & an Account of Newspapers*. New York: Weathervane Books, 1970.
Thompson, C. Seymour. *Evolution of the American Public Library: 1653–1876*. Washington, DC: Scarecrow Press, 1952.
Tolles, Frederick B. *Meeting House and County House: The Quaker Merchants of Colonial Philadelphia, 1682–1763*. New York: University of North Carolina Press, 1948; reprint, New York: W. W. Norton & Company, 1963.
———. *George Logan of Philadelphia*. New York: Oxford University Press, 1953.
Tully, Alan. *Forming American Politics: Ideals, Interests, and Institutions in Colonial New York and Pennsylvania*. Baltimore, MD: The Johns Hopkins University Press, 1994.
———. *William Penn's Legacy: Politics and Social Structure in Provincial Pennsylvania, 1726–1755*. Baltimore, MD: The Johns Hopkins University Press, 1977.
Warner, Michael. *The Letter of the Republic: Publication and the Public Sphere in Eighteenth-Century America*. Cambridge, MA: Harvard University Press, 1990.
Weiss, Harry B. *A Graphic Summary of the Growth of Newspapers in New York and Other States, 1704–1820*. New York: New York Public Library, 1948.
Wells, Robert V. *The Population of the British Colonies inAmerican before 1776: A Survey of Census Data*. Princeton, NJ: Princeton University Press, 1975.
Wheeler, Joseph Towne. *The Maryland Press 1777–1790*. Baltimore, MD: The Maryland Historical Society, 1938.
Wilson, Kathleen. *The Sense of the People: Politics, Culture and Imperialism in England, 1715–1785*. Cambridge: Cambridge University Press, 1995, 1998.
Wolf, Edwin. *The Book Culture of a Colonial American City: Philadelphia Books, Bookmen, and Booksellers*. Oxford: Clarendon Press, 1988.
Wood, George A. *William Shirley: Governor of Massachusetts, 1741–1756 A History*. New York: Columbia University, 1920.
Wood, Gordon. *The Creation of the American Republic 1776–1787*. New York: W. W. Norton & Company, 1969.

———. *The Radicalism of the American Revolution*. New York: Vintage Books, 1991.
Wright, Esmond. *Franklin of Philadelphia*. Cambridge, MA: The Belknap Press of Harvard University Press, 1986.
Wroth, Lawrence. *An American Bookshelf 1755*. New York: Arno Press & The New York Times, 1969.
———. *A History of Printing in Colonial Maryland 1686–1776*. Baltimore, MD: Typothetae of Baltimore, 1922.
———. *The Colonial Printer*. Charlottesville, VA: The University Press of Virginia, 1964.
Zuckert, Michael P. *Natural Rights and the New Republicanism*. Princeton, NJ: Princeton University Press, 1994.

PUBLISHED SECONDARY SOURCES: JOURNAL ARTICLES

Bulloch, J. M. "Thomas Gordon the Independent Whig." *Aberdeen University Library Bulletin*, Vol. III., Nos. 17, 18, (1918), 3–33.
Dill, William A. "Growth of Newspapers in the United States," *Published as a Bulletin by the Department of Journalism* (April 1928), 1–80.
Hallenbeck, Chester T. "A Colonial Reading List." *The Pennsylvania Magazine of History and Biography*, Vol. LVI, No. 4 (1932), 289–340.
Hamowy, Ronald. "Cato's Letters, John Locke, and the Republican Paradigm." *History of Political Thought*, Vol. XI. No.2 (Summer 1990), 273–294.
Jacobson, D. L. "Thomas Gordon's Works of Tacitus in Pre-Revolutionary America." *Bulletin of The New York Public Library*, Volume 69 (January–December 1965), 58–65.
Kaestle, Carl F. "The Public Reaction to John Dickinson's Farmer's Letters," *Proceedings of the American Antiquarian Society*, Volume 78 (Worcester, MA: American Antiquarian Society, 1969), 322–359.
Kramnick, Isaac. "Republican Revisionism," *The American Historical Review*, Volume 87, Issue 3 (June, 1982), 629–664.
Liddle, William D. "'A Patriot King, or None': Lord Bolingbroke and the American Renunciation of George III." *The Journal of American History*, Volume 65, Issue 4 (Mar., 1979), 951–970.
Lundberg, David and Henry F. May. "The Enlightened Reader In America." *American Quarterly*, Volume 28, Issue 2 (Summer, 1976), 262–293.
Lutz, Donald S. "The Relative Influence of European Writers on Late Eighteenth-Century American Political Thought." *The American Political Science Review*, Volume 78, Issue 1 (Mar., 1984), 189–197.
McDonald, Forrest. "A Founding Father's Library." *Literature of Liberty*. Volume 1, Issue 1 (January/March, 1978) 1–14.
Pocock, J. G. A. "Machiavelli, Harrington and English Political Ideologies in the Eighteenth Century." *William and Mary Quarterly*, Third Series, Volume 22, Issue 4 (Oct., 1965), 549–583.

Realey, C. B. "The London Journal and Its Authors 1720–1723." *University of Kansas Humanistic Studies*, Volume V (1936), 1–38.
Schwoerer, Lois G. "The Literature of the Standing Army Controversy, 1697–1699." *The Huntington Library Quarterly*, Volume XXXVIII, Number 3 (May 1965), 187–212.
Shalhope, Robert E. "Republicanism and Early American Historiography." *William and Mary Quarterly*, Third Series, Volume 39, Issue 2 (Apr., 1982), 334–356.
——. "Toward a Republican Synthesis: The Emergence of an Understanding of Republicanism in American Historiography." *William and Mary Quarterly*, Third Series, Volume 28, Issue 1 (January 1972), 49–80.
Weiss, Harry B. "A Graphic Summary of the Growth of Newspapers in New York and Other States 1704–1820," *Bulletin of the New York Public Library* (April 1948), 3–17.

UNPUBLISHED SECONDARY SOURCES

Edgar, Walter Bellingrath. "The Libraries of Colonial South Carolina" (Doctoral dissertation, University of South Carolina, 1969).
McMahon, Marie Patricia. "The Quiet and Stability of this Free State" (Doctoral dissertation, American University, 1986).

Index

Adams, Samuel, 55–56
Addison, Joseph, 16, 23n20, 28–29, 67, 75, 106
Alexander, James, 64, 69–70, 79n9
Allen, James, 56
American Mutiny Act. *See* Quartering Act
American Revolution, 6, 8, 78, 103–11, 115
American Weekly Mercury (AWM), *33–34*, 59n22, 85–87, *118*, *122–26*, *130–32*
Amsterdam, 15, 19, 21, 23n10
Anglican Church. *See* Church of England
anticlericalism, 14–15
Appleby, Joyce, 5
arbitrary government, 14, 35–36, 55, 57–58, 70, 89, 92, 95
Atterbury, Francis. *See* Atterbury plot
Atterbury plot, 18–19, 24n33, 25n35

backcountry, 41, 46n76
Bailyn, Bernard, 2, 79n2, 81n43
balanced government, 5, 22, 51, 105
Bangorian Controversy, 14
Banning, Lance, 2
Bible, 15, 29, 39
Bolingbroke, Viscount, 10n21, 16, 28, 55, 58

Boston Evening Post, *33*, 55, 60n25, *122, 125, 128*
Boston Gazette, 40, 106
Boston Gazette and Country Journal, *33–34*, 58, *119*, *122–23*, *128*
Boston News Letter, 54, 59n20, *119*, *126, 128*
Boston Weekly News Letter, 59n20
Bradford, Andrew, 59n22, 86–96, 98n1, 99n8, 101n41
Bradford, William, 64, 66–67, 79n7, 98n8
Bradford, William III, 96, 107–8
Breen, T. H., 7
Breintnall, Joseph, 92, 101n49
British Journal, 16, 23n19
Brutus (from antiquity), 71, 104, 112n37, *122, 124, 129, 130*
Bushman, Richard, 51
Busy-Body Series, 92, 101n49

Cadwalader, Jacob, 29
Caesar, Julius, 16, 40, 71, 76, 112n37
Cato's Letters: in British North America, 2, 7, 22, 27–34, 36–39, 103–11, 114, *118–32;* in Europe, 19, 21; in London, 1, 19–21; in Massachusetts, 51–58; in New York, 62–79; in Pennsylvania, 41, 85–98; in South Carolina, 43

Cato the Younger, 16
The Censor, 46n68
Charles-Town Library Society, 28–29
Checkley, John, 52
Church of England (Anglican Church), 1, 15, 39, 54, 72, 75–76, 83, 93, 97
Church of Rome. *See* Roman Catholicism
civic humanism, 3–4
Clark, Charles, 6, 80n26
clergy, 15, 39, 74–75, *126, 128, 131–32;* Anglican, 52, 54, 74–75; Roman Catholic, 19, 40, 96
Clinton, George, 84n103
Colbourn, Trevor, 28
College of New Jersey library, 28
Collins, Anthony, 22n9
commonweal, 3–4, 17–18, 21, 31
commonwealthmen, 3–4. *See also* Real Whigs
Connecticut Gazette, 109
Cook, Elizabeth Christine, 2
corruption, 3–4, 52–53, 55, 76–78, 88–90, 104, *122, 128–31;* in government, 5, 16, 18, 20, 64–65, 91, 94–95, 109–10; of government officials, 17, 31–32, 40, 56, 67, 70; of the populace, 17, 21, 106, *122*
Cosby, William, 62–64, 66, 68–72, 77, 79n9, 81n49
Country Party, 4–5, 7, 10n21
Court Party, 4–5, 10n21, 26n44, 38, 46n59
covenant, 39, 54, 59n18
The Craftsman, 10n21, 16, 55, 58, 60n28, 106
Criton, 19
Currency Act, 107

Davis, Richard, 30
DeLancey, James, 63, 69, 76
D'Holbach, Baron, 21
Dickinson, James, 108–11. See also *Letters from a Farmer in Pennsylvania*
Discourses upon Tacitus. See Gordon's *Tacitus*

Dodsley, Robert, 29
Douglass, William, 55
Draper, John, 60n26
Dryden, 66, 73

Edes, Benjamin, 58
Edgar, Walter, 29
English Bill of Rights, 35, 45n37, 108
Episcopal Church, 74–75. *See also* Church of England

factions: danger of, 21, 73, 100n26, *125, 130–32;* political, 4, 6, 37, 51, 62, 72, 79n2, 89; in Zenger trial 63–64, 66, 70
flattery, 38, 53, 89, 94, *123, 128–29*
Fleet, Thomas, 55, 60n25
Fowle, Daniel, 55
France, 17, 21–22, 38
Franklin, Benjamin, 52–53, 90, 94–96, 101n41
Franklin, James, 52
freedom of press, 2, 35, 68, 74–75, 83n85, 97, 105–6; to keep government free, 32, 64–65, 69; to keep government officials in check, 31–32, 67–69, 78, 91
freedom of speech, 34, 51–53, 64, 103–6; in British North America, 31, 33, 95–97, *122, 128–31;* in *Cato's Letters*, 2, 20, 33, 55, 58, 64, 78; to keep government officials in check, 17–18, 31–35, 51, 71–72, 91; in Zenger trial, *34,* 44n32, 45n32, 67–69, 106
free government, 31, 44n21, 53, 65, 67–71, 91, *124, 132;* in England, 5, 16–17; philosophy of, 17, 19–20, 33, 35–36, 55, 94–96; preservation of, 17–18, 32
French Revolution, 21–22

Gaine, Hugh, 73–75
Galloway, Joseph, 108, 112n39
Georgia Gazette, 109
Gill, John, 58
Goddard, William, 108

Gordon, Patrick, 86, 90, 100n37
Gordon's *Tacitus*, 1, 20–21, 27–30, 40, 43n12, 65–66, 80n22, *118*
Greece, ancient, 90; Sparta, 56
Green, Bartholomew, 54
Grenville, George, 105, 111n12
Guardian, 29

Habermas, Jurgen, 6
Hall, David, 30
Hamilton, Andrew: in New York (Zenger Trial), 44n32, 69–70, 81n49, 92, 98n4; in Pennsylvania, 86, 90, 92–93, 100n39, 101n41
Harley, Robert, 17, 24n27
Harrington, James, 3, 28
Harvard library, 28
Heath, Joseph, 56
Henry III of France, 38
Hoadly, Benjamin, 14
Hobbes, Thomas, 3, 9n11, 28
Holt, John, 32, 45n32, 104–6
honor, 38, 52–53, 65–66, 75, 90, 104, *128*
human nature, 4, 18, *130, 132*; discussion in British North America, 31, 36–37, 52–56, 67–68, 73, 86, 88–91, 106; discussion in *Cato's Letters*, 37, 53–56, *122, 128*; discussion in Gordon's *Tacitus*, 20–21, 40
The Humorist, 14
Hutchinson, Thomas, 104

Independent Advertiser, *34*, 55–57, 61n42, *119, 123–24, 128*
Independent Reflector, *33–34*, 39, 72–77, 83n85, *122–26, 130*
Independent Whig, 1, 14–16, 19–21, 22n7, 23n10; reprinted in British North American newspapers, 9n11, 27–30, 39, 43n1, 43n12, 46n68, 52, 54, 62, 72–77, 98n1, *118*
Ireland, 13, 15, 73

Jacobites, 15–16, 18–19, 24n33
Jacobitism, 14–15
James II, 15, 18

Keimer, Samuel, 43n1, 100n40
Keith, George, 99n8
Keith, William, 86–87
King's College (now Columbia), 62, 73–77
Kramnick, Isaac, 5

Letters from a Farmer in Pennsylvania, 32, 103, 108–10, 114
Levy, Leonard, 2
libel, 35, 66–68, 87; "Discourses upon Libels," 68, 91, *125*; false, 35, 52, 91; "Reflections on libeling," 33, 67, *122, 129;* seditious libel, 8, 52, 68, 70, 79n7, 80n26, 81n49, 87, 92, 99
liberalism. See Lockean Liberalism
libertarian, 3–4. See also Lockean Liberalism
liberty, 1, 16, 19, 34–36, 56–58, 64–67, 71–72, 74, 76–78, 88–96, 106–10, *124–25, 128–32*; British liberty, 5, 8, 17–18, 20, 100n26; public liberty, 13, 20, 33, 39, 45n32, 53–54, 58, 96, 104. See also freedom of press, freedom of speech, free government
Library Company of Philadelphia, 28
Livingston, William, 72, 76, 83n88, 84n103
Lockean Liberalism, 3–5, 71
Locke, John, 2–4, 23n9, 28–29, 97. See also Lockean Liberalism
London Journal, 16, 19, 23n19, 25n37, 53
Lundberg, David, 27–28

Machiavelli, Niccolo, 97
Maier, Pauline, 2
Maryland Gazette, 109
Massachusetts Gazette, 59n20
Massachusetts Spy, *33*, 103–4, 111n3, *122–25, 128–29*
Mather, Cotton, 52
May, Henry, 27–28
McDonald, Forrest, 2
militias, 105
monarchy, 13, 15, 18–20, 22, 40, 51, 73, 78, 95

monopolies, 17–18, 31, 78
Montesquieu, Baron, 28
Morning Chronicle, 106
Morrisites, 64
Morris, Lewis, 63–64, 66, 70–72

Nash, Gary, 2
New England Courant, *33*, 39, 42, 52, 59n11, *122–23*, *128*
New Hampshire Gazette, *125*, *129*
New Jersey Library Company, 28
Newport Mercury, *119*
newspapers: importance of, 6–8, 22, 27, 30–43, 85–86, 90, 97–98, 113–14; opposition, 51, 55, 58, 103, 115; Revolutionary Era, 103, 109–10, 114; in Zenger Trial, 63, 77. *See also* individual titles of newspapers
New York Gazette (*NYG*), 62–64, 67–68, 74–75, 77, 98n8, *118*, *122*, *130*
New York Journal or General Advertiser (*NYJ*), 32, *33–34*, 45n32, 104–6, *122–25*, *130*
New York Mercury, 40, 73–76, 83n85, *118*, *122*, *130*
New York Society Library, 28
New York Weekly Journal (*NYWJ*), *33–34*, 40–42, 45n32, 62–71, 77, *122–26*, *129–30*

Pamela, 29
Parker, James, 74, 83n80
Parliament, 13–14, 17–18, 35, 103, 107–8, 114, *125*, *132*
Pennsylvania Chronicle and Universal Advertiser, 108, 112n39, *119*
Pennsylvania Evening Post, *34*, *124–25*
Pennsylvania Gazette, *33–34*, 40, 85–86, 90, 94, 100n40, *118–19*, *122–26*, *132*
Pennsylvania Journal, 32, *33–34*, 45n32, 85, 96–97, 107–8, *119*, *122*, *124–25*, *132*
Penn, William, 86, 98n5, 100n37
plagiarism, 75, 77
Pocock, J. G. A., 4–5
Pope, Alexander, 28

Protestant: countries, 16, 36, 57, 89; dissenters, 15
public good, 4, 17–18, 56, 73, 88–89, 92, 105, 108
public sphere, 6–7, 97
public spirit, 36, 57, 86, 88–90, 94, *123*, *128*, *131–32*
Puritans, 29, 52, 54, 59n6

Quakers, 86–87, 93, 97, 99, 101n41, 112n39
Quartering Act, 105, 107

Real Whigs, 3–4, 10n21, 16. *See also* commonwealthmen
Redwood Library of Newport Rhode Island, 28
Rees, Margret, 29
religious zealots, 93
republican, 5–6, 16, 51, 78
republicanism, 3, 5–6
reverence, 38, 65, 90, *126*, *129–31*
Rhode Island College library, 28
Richardson, Samuel, 29
Robbins, Caroline, 3–4
Rogers, Gamaliel, 55
Roman Catholicism, 1, 15, 18–19, 21–22, 39, 46n57, 54, 81n48, 89
Roman Cato, 16, 60n25, 106
Rome, ancient, 35, 40, 65, 71, 76–77, 94
rotation in office, 82n59, 92, 94

Sallust, 1, 21, 27–28, 43n12
Scheme, Peter, 68
Schutz, John, 55
Scott, John Morin, 72
Scourge, Humphey, 97
Shirley, William, 51, 55–56
Shute, Samuel, 52
Sidney, Algernon, 3, 28, 37, 45n57, 56–57, 61n42, 69, 81n48, 97, 108
Silence Dogood, 52. *See also* Benjamin Franklin
slavery, 36, 38, 65, 71–72, *124*
smallpox, inoculation, 52
Smith, William Jr., 72

Smith, William Sr., 64, 69–70, 72
South America, 17, 24n27
South Carolina Gazette, *33–34*, 42–43, 113, *122–23, 125, 132*
South-Sea Bubble Crisis, 17–18, 78, 99n15
South-Sea Stock Company, 16–18
Spectator, 29, 60n28, 67, 75
Stamp Act, 109
standing army, 1, 13–15, 20, 104–5, 109–10, 111n12, *125, 130*
Steele, Robert, 29, 67
stock companies, 17, 20, 31. *See also* South-Sea Company and South-Sea Bubble Crisis
Switzerland, 40; Geneva, 21

Tacitus. See Gordon's *Tacitus*
taxes, 51, 58, 73, 82n68, 87, 103–10, *122, 132*
Thomas, Isaiah, 103–4, 111n3
Tories, 16–17, 19, 23n21, 37, 103, 111n4
Tyng, John, 56
tyrannical government, 35, 57, 65
tyranny, 36, 39, 54, 57, 65, 75, 77, 89, 94, 96

Union Library of Hatboro in Pennsylvania, 28–29

Van Dam, Rip, 63, 69–70
Virginia Gazette, 42, 109
virtue, 1, 4–5, 16, 38, 72, 76–77, 94; in British North America, 31, 53, *124–25, 130–31;* in *Cato's Letters*, 18, 35, 38, 53, 65, 106
Voltaire, 21

Walpole, Robert, 16, 19–20, 80n22
Warner, Michael, 6
The Watchman, 96
Weekly Rehearsal (Boston), 55, 60n25
Wharton, Thomas, 108, 112n39
Whigs, 3–4, 16, 37, 103
Wilson, Kathleen, 7

Yale library, 28

Zenger, John Peter, 63–71, 77, 90; background of, 64; trial of, 32, *34*, 44n32, 69–71, 81n49, 92, 106–7, *124, 130, 132*

www.ingramcontent.com/pod-product-compliance
Lightning Source LLC
Chambersburg PA
CBHW030115010526
44116CB00005B/252